ILLINOIS CENTRAL
Monday Mornin' Rails

BY JIM BOYD
Photography by the author except as noted

ANDOVER
JUNCTION
PUBLICATIONS
P.O. BOX 1160   ANDOVER, NJ 07821

". . . Ride their fathers' magic carpets made of steel . . ."

To my good friend, Chester E. French

EDITORIAL DIRECTOR: Joyce C. Mooney
PUBLISHER: Stephen A. Esposito
EDITORIAL AND ART DIRECTOR: Mike Schafer

ACKNOWLEDGMENTS: I would like to thank the following people for their help in preparing this book. Chet French dug into his archives and memory for details and data and was a great help in sorting things out. The information he uncovered on the history of the Dixon "River Track" has never been previously published. Traveling Engineer Parky Parkman remembered our trip on the Tallahatchie District like it was yesterday and was an excellent source of information. Mike McBride was generous in supplying his photos and in answering numerous questions about Dixon's geography. Burlington Northern engineer John H. Johnson of Birmingham, Alabama, supplied data on the Frisco over Adamsville Mountain, and Bruce Meyer of EMD confirmed my data on the performance of the SD40A's. Bruce and Parker Lamb supplied their black-and-white steam photos, and John Szwajkart and Howard Patrick provided vintage slides. Thanks to Skip Gage for the Wayne A. Johnston portrait and Jim Folk for the dustjacket portrait. IC historian Al Lind was most helpful, as were Jim Kubajak and Charles Werner of the IC Historical Society. Jerry Pyfer and John Fredrickson of the North Western Illinois Chapter-NRHS supplied newsletters containing much timely information, and Lee Hastman's roster information proved instrumental to fact-checking. And special thanks goes to Don McFall, who suggested the idea of an IC photo book in the first place. Of course, publishers Joyce Mooney and Steve Esposito made this all possible, and it was a great pleasure to work with my long-time friend Mike Schafer in creating a book out of materials and memories that we often shared trackside. Mike knows many aspects of the IC better than I, and it is not by mere chance that he shows up in the photo on the title page.—*Jim Boyd*

FRONT COVER PHOTO: Brakeman Jim Boyd was rolling south on meat train CC-6 in September 1970 at 53rd Street (Hyde Park), as No. 7, the *Illini*, overtook them on Track 1 before slowing for its 63rd Street station stop. The lead E9 on No. 7 was 2039, formerly Florida East Coast 1034, which IC had purchased second hand from that carrier. **TITLE PAGE:** Westbound 13, the *Land O' Corn*, had just met CC-6 at Case Siding in Rockford, Illinois, and was easing back onto the main in October 1966 as Mike Schafer, in his Rockford East High School "E-Rab" jacket, managed to get into the picture. **THIS PAGE:** The northbound *City of New Orleans* was viewed from Traveling Engineer Elliott G. Parkman's office in Memphis Central Station on August 13, 1969. **CONTENTS PAGE:** One of IC's two remaining slant-nose E6's, 4001, was eastbound on the *Land O' Corn* just west of Rockford on April 12, 1965. **BACK COVER PHOTO:** In May 1960, 2-10-2 2739 was stored serviceable in the Paducah roundhouse, ready for a call that would never come.

INTRODUCTION

Wayne A. Johnston's Railroad

CONSERVATIVE: That's a one-word definition for the Illinois Central Railroad in its centennial year of 1951. President Wayne A. Johnston was running a company that took pride in its passenger trains and professed an enduring faith in the coal-burning steam locomotive. The "Main Line of Mid-America" was a north-south railroad in a country full of east-west railroads. Its primary purpose in life was to link Chicago with New Orleans, spreading out along the way to cover the rich Mississippi River bottomlands, reach into the Kentucky coalfields and stretch an outward hand to western connections at Omaha.

Diesel-powered streamliners were breathtaking in orange and chocolate, while workhorse passenger trains packed people and parcels into green heavyweight cars pulled by fast 4-8-2's and 4-6-2's. Bananas from New Orleans and grain from Iowa flowed into Chicago behind husky 4-8-2's spawned in the company's Paducah Shops, and bituminous coal rumbled out of Kentucky behind 2-10-2's. Throughout the system, Mikados with steamboat whistles trundled the main and branch lines to provide the local service that laced the railroad into the very fabric of the community and countryside. IC had the look of a traditional railroad, from centered Pyle National headlights (with visors) to red cabooses with kerosene marker lamps.

A company of rich and proud heritage, Illinois Central could trace its beginnings to an era well before the Civil War, when Illinois was still threatened by the rebellious Sauk Indian Chief Black Hawk, Fort Dearborn on Lake Michigan had not yet become Chicago,

Galena was the state's most important "industrial" center with its lead mines, and Cairo, at the confluence of the Ohio and Mississippi rivers, was the state's center of commerce. Within five years of the successful operation of the *John Bull* steam locomotive on New Jersey's Camden & Amboy in 1831, prairie folks were already talking about a great "Central Railroad" running the length of Illinois.

Senator Stephen A. Douglas got a federal land grant bill through Congress in 1850 which led directly to the Illinois legislature authorizing the construction of the Illinois Central Railroad on February 10, 1851. The railroad was to reach north from Cairo to Centralia where it would split, with one line going north and west to Galena and Dunleith (now East Dubuque) and the other angling northeast to Chicago. When these "Charter Lines" were completed in 1856, the IC was—at 705 miles—the longest railroad in the world and contained completely within the borders of Illinois.

After one of its corporate lawyers, Abraham Lincoln, had become president of the United States, IC went on to provide valuable service to the Union during the Civil War. Following the war, the railroad began to expand by acquiring existing railroads, reaching first to Sioux City, Iowa, on the Missouri River in 1870 and then south to New Orleans in 1873. Other lines off the main stem soon filled out the system. The new Ohio River bridge at Cairo in 1890 and the Chicago-Freeport link to the western Charter Line in 1891 made the basic IC system map nearly complete.

On May 30, 1883, a young New York banker named Edward H. Harriman had been elected

WITH A CLASSIC IC consist of E-units, streamlined cars and modernized heavyweights, No. 101-53, the connection for the *City of New Orleans* and *City of Miami*, departed St. Louis Union Station, bound for Carbondale in June 1963.

to the IC board of directors, and he had a considerable influence on the railroad in the decades that followed, for unlike the "robber barons" of his era, Harriman believed in solid investment and quality management. By 1908 his empire also included Union Pacific, Southern Pacific, Chicago & Alton and Central of Georgia as well as the Erie. As a result, the IC entered the 1920's with numerous steam locomotives (2-8-0's, 2-8-2's and a few 4-6-2's) and passenger cars built to the Harriman "Common Standard" designs.

By the end of the 1920's, the IC was truly the "Main Line of Mid-America," an industrial giant with a double-track main line, a state-of-the-art electrified suburban service in Chicago, fast 4-8-2's for manifest and passenger trains and immense USRA* heavy 2-10-2's for coal and drag freight. Thanks to a rebuilding and upgrading program within its huge Paducah (Kentucky) backshop over the next couple of decades, IC would enter the diesel era with essentially the same steam locomotives that had seen it through the Great Depression.

*The United States Railway Administration, which controlled most U.S. rail operations during the World War I period.

For a railroad that would be one of the very last to run steam, IC was one of the very first to buy diesels when it acquired two GE/Ingersoll-Rand box-cab switchers in 1929. By 1936 it rostered 15 diesel switchers and three huge transfer freight units in addition to the articulated *Green Diamond* streamliner used between Chicago and St. Louis. In 1940 IC bought its first General Motors E6 passenger diesel for the new *City of Miami*; the unit wore a unique orange-and-green "bow wave" paint scheme. In 1941, the E6-powered *Panama Limited* streamliner was introduced in a beautiful orange-and-chocolate livery designed by Paul Meyer of General Motors' Art & Colour Industrial Design Department in Detroit. This "Panama scheme" would become IC's standard livery for its passenger fleet, and the overnight all-Pullman *Panama Limited* between Chicago and New Orleans would gain a reputation as one of America's finest passenger trains.

Meanwhile, Paducah Shops were rebuilding and upgrading IC's steam locomotives. In its most significant program, Paducah used new 70-inch drivers and one-piece cast underframes to turn World War I 2-10-2's into fast

and powerful 2500-series 4-8-2's, and in 1942-43 it even built 20 nearly identical but brand-new 4-8-2's in the 2600 series. The Paducah rebuildings touched almost every locomotive in the fleet, from Pacifics to Mikados to switch engines, bringing the railroad out of the 1940's with an excellent stable of modern motive power custom-tailored to its needs.

Even with all this in-house surgery and creativity, the IC was severely conservative in its steam philosophy by testing and then pointedly ignoring such modern appliances as feedwater heaters and boosters. IC steam was plain, raw, coal-burning power painted all-business black with only oxide-red cab roofs and big white numbers on the tenders for decoration. But the philosophy worked well, and by 1951 IC was still handling *all* of its road freight behind steam, and the company's first true road freight diesel, GP7 8950, was only two months on the property.

By delaying freight dieselization until the early 1950's, IC had avoided the mix-'n'-match motive-power chaos of "covered wagon" units from a myriad of manufacturers. Adorned in IC's traditional black-and-white diesel switcher livery that dated from 1939, the utilitarian and versatile "Geep" from the Electro-Motive Division of General Motors was the machine

that would displace the modern Paducah steam from the IC—but not until 1960 would the job be completely done!

Back in 1919, a farm boy from Champaign County had graduated from the University of Illinois and taken a job as an accountant on the IC. Over the years Wayne A. Johnston worked his way up through the company, learning the railroad from one end to the other. At the peak of the Second World War, on February 23, 1945, at 46 years of age, he became president of the IC. As the former general traffic agent for mail, baggage and express, he knew and respected the passenger business, and as the former superintendent of the Kentucky Division, he knew the importance of a loyal coal-burning, steam-powered railroad to the miners around Dawson Springs and the workers in the Paducah Shops. His powerful personality was reflected in the postwar character of the entire railroad.

During Illinois Central's centennial year of 1951, President Wayne A. Johnston was presiding over a prosperous, progressive and traditional railroad. That same year I turned age ten and was watching IC trains that paraded past my dining room window in Dixon, Illinois. I was just old enough to realize that the Illinois Central was "my" railroad. ✌

WAYNE A. JOHNSTON was president of the IC from 1945 through 1966, and his strong personality kept the railroad firmly rooted in conservatism.
—FABIAN BACHRACH/ICRR He firmly believed that passenger service should be the pride of the company, and the image of a shiny E8 on the westbound *Land O' Corn* (top) meeting black GP9's on a freight beneath the Winnebago Street bridge in Rockford, Illinois, in May 1965 is a classic of his era.

CHAPTER 1

The Home Road

They say that you can choose your friends, but you're stuck with your relatives. The same thing applies to hometowns. Few of us had any choice in where we were born or raised—or where we saw our first trains.

As hometowns go, I guess I was pretty lucky. Dixon, Illinois, population at that time of 11,600, was 100 miles west of Chicago, where the double-tracked Chicago & North Western main line to Omaha crossed over the Freeport-to-Clinton, Illinois, line of the Illinois Central. Both railroads had small yards on the south side of town and shared some interesting industrial trackage.

My earliest memories of trains are of big, black steam engines and fast-moving yellow streamliners at the North Western depot, viewed from behind the zebra-striped barriers at the edge of the parking lot. A visit to the depot was always considered high adventure at a time when my world was limited to a couple of blocks in any direction from our house at the west end of Second Street, safely out of reach of any railroad tracks.

But in 1949, when I was eight years old, we moved to a new house that my folks had built at 620 First Avenue on the north side. The house sat atop a small hill and overlooked the Illinois Central. Our big dining room window had a clear view of the tracks on an embankment about a block away. The IC was 100 percent steam and saw a half dozen trains in daytime with about four more overnight. The nearby Squires Avenue crossing gave the engineers ample reason to exercise those beautiful steamboat whistles, and the northbound climb out of the Rock River valley made for great

stack talk as the freights came over the river bridge and opened up for the assault on the hill.

There were seven grade crossings northward from Squires Avenue, each separated by only one city block. Most engineers would "gang up" their whistle signals and stretch out each warning over two or three crossings. One particular engineer had a beautiful and distinctive style that I always listened for. He would never quite let up on the whistle cord and would string all seven of those two-longs-a-short-and-a-long together in one wonderful undulating melody. The last time I heard that on a steam whistle was sometime in 1951.

Most of the locomotives looked pretty much alike, except for the switcher that would go by once or twice a day. About four blocks south of our house lived Grandma and Grandpa Boyd, and their back yard bordered on a Borden Company spur track where that switcher would spend a couple of hours working every afternoon. In my first real ventures to "seek out" trains, I would go down to Grandpa Boyd's in hopes of seeing the switcher.

Up to this time I was just another kid in grade school, and my interest in trains was pretty much a solitary thing; nobody else was particularly interested in them. One day in the summer of 1953, however, things took a dramatic change. I went down to Grandpa Boyd's to watch the switch engine and found somebody else sitting on my favorite pile of ties. It was Chet French, and he liked trains too. He was two years older than I and about to enter high school, and he knew a lot more than I did about railroads.

We struck up an immediate friendship, and I got a quick education in train operations,

THE "PUZZLE SWITCH" between the North House track and the connection to the C&NW was a distinctive feature of the yard at Dixon, Illinois. In July 1962, GP9 9157 was idling next to the freight station during a lull in the day's work.

MIKADO 1519 was rambling southward over the Squires Avenue crossing on the north side of Dixon in 1953. This was typical motive power on the Springfield Division during the early 1950's. The Boyd home was a city block west of here, and the curve ahead of the locomotive was readily visible from the house. About a half mile ahead, just north of the Rock River bridge, was the Borden Company spur (below) where 0-6-0 313 was working in 1953 in this view from Grandpa Boyd's back yard.

AUTHOR JIM BOYD was 15 years old when this photo (right) was taken on the front step of the house at 620 First Avenue in 1956. Chet French (below right) was posing in the cab of the 313 as it waited across from the high school at the west end of River Street in 1953. Jim and Chet had met just a few months earlier that year while watching the 0-6-0 switch the Borden plant.

wheel arrangements and engine numbers. A typical summer afternoon thereafter would find us working on my American Flyer S-gauge model railroad and indulging in two-man baseball games (an avid Chicago Cubs fan, Chet knew the line-ups of every National League team). A whistle would propel us to the back yard or dining room window to watch the passing train.

I learned that this was the Amboy District of the Springfield Division and that it was known as the "Gruber," a name whose origins are lost in obscurity (although some theorize it was a mutation of the Civil War-era nickname "Goober Line," as in peanuts). It was one of IC's two original charter lines and was built in 1855 from Centralia to Galena and Dunleith (now East Dubuque), Illinois. In 1953, crews operated out of Freeport, 35 miles to the north, and ran to Clinton, 130 miles to the south.

Chet had gotten ahold of the March 1953 *Trains & Travel* Magazine which contained a photo roster of IC steam power, and from it we learned that the Gruber was populated mostly with Mikados. There were two distinctive types: The 1200's through 1600's were Harriman standard 2-8-2's that had been modernized in the Paducah Shops, while the bigger 2100's were similar Mikes rebuilt with cutdown 2-10-2 frames and cylinders. Chet informed me that the IC referred to their engine types simply by numbers, whereas C&NW, on the other side of town, used "class" designations (Class E 4-6-2's, Class E4 streamlined

4-6-4's and Class H 4-8-4's, for example).

Because of the amount of local industry in town, Dixon had a resident IC switch engine, an 0-6-0, which would be rotated to Freeport once a month for maintenance. The 341 was Dixon's regular engine, and it would swap off with the 313, 259 and 275 as needed. The run to Bordens and "The Colony" (the state mental hospital north of town which got coal for its power plant) would bring the 0-6-0 galloping past my back yard almost every afternoon.

Once Chet had taught me to watch engine numbers and identify wheel arrangements—and after that *Trains & Travel* article revealed the potential of the locomotive fleet—it became great sport to catch anything different. One of my biggest thrills was 2-10-2 No. 2810 on November 11, 1954 (many years later I would learn it was on a southbound Dunbar ore train bound for St. Louis off the Chicago Great Western at South Freeport, called "Dun-

bar" on the IC). I spotted the 1002, an odd little low-drivered 4-6-2, dead in tow, headed for Cherokee, Iowa, and 2-8-0 791 came into town once on a work train.

When that 2-8-0 was in Dixon, Chet and I were hoping that it would venture over to the north side. One day somebody told Chet that it would be heading back to Freeport that evening, and we stood on the bluff overlooking IC's handsome Rock River deck-girder trestle in hopes of catching it. We could see two headlights working over in the yard. We knew one was probably the 0-6-0, but the other just might be that 2-8-0. Well after dark, a few whistle blasts and a loud exhaust announced that one of those engines was coming our way. We were bitterly disappointed to see the 1299, the regular Mikado on the local, come storming past us, making his run for the hill. (Disappointed! What either of us would give to see the 1299 come across that bridge today.)

MIKADO 1299 was a regular engine through Dixon in the mid-1950's, about the time this photo (right) **was made at the Freeport roundhouse. Behind the 1299 is the tender of 3962, one of two Paducah-rebuilt former Vicksburg, Shreveport & Pacific light 2-8-2's that were assigned to the Madison branch and made trips on the Gruber.—C.C. GRAYSON Sister 3969 is shown** (below) **on October 5, 1952. —CHARLES T. FELSTEAD**

A pair of unusually small 2-8-2's had been showing up on the noon locals. Since these weren't shown in the *Trains & Travel* article, it would be much later before I would understand that the 3962 and 3969 were rebuilds of Vicksburg, Shreveport & Pacific locomotives (as was the 1002) that had gone through IC's Paducah backshop; they had been working the Freeport-Madison (Wisconsin) branch until they were replaced by dual-controlled GP7's 8850 and 8851 in 1952.

Every kid has his favorite engine, and mine was the 2134. One day in 1953 my dad had offered to drive his Uncle Art down to Mendota (28 miles south of Dixon) to catch the *California Zephyr*, and I went along. I don't remember the *Zephyr* at all, but on the way home in Uncle Art's Cadillac just above Mendota, we pulled alongside a northbound IC freight powered by the 2134. Dad gave in to my obvious excitement and drove alongside the locomotive at about 45 m.p.h. all the way up through Sublette to Amboy where the tracks swing away from U.S. 52. The big Mike had put on an incredible show, and I had watched the fireman

A MEMORABLE chase alongside the 2134 north of Mendota in 1953 made this big Mikado the author's all-time favorite. It is shown at Clinton, Illinois, in the early 1950's. The 2100's were older 2-8-2's that had been rebuilt at Paducah using the shortened frames and big cylinders from 2-10-2's which had given their boilers to the new 2500-series 4-8-2's.—C.C. GRAYSON

riding easily in the bouncing cab. It was the first time I'd ever paced a moving train, and I'll never forget it. When we got home I ran out to the Squires Avenue crossing and was able to watch "my" 2134 hammering around the curve. It was awesome, just awesome.

So there I was in the summer of 1953 with a friend who knew about trains and a railroad full of steam locomotives right outside my dining-room window. But with knowledge came curiosity, and I was anxious to expand my world. A bicycle soon took care of that.

Operations in Dixon

Dixon was separated by the east-west running Rock River into the "north side" and

"south side," and kids stayed pretty much in their own neighborhoods. The Chicago & North Western was a far bigger, busier and more-colorful operation than the IC, but it was "way over on the south side" and for all practical purposes out of reach until I got my bicycle in 1954. But by then, the IC had solidly become my favorite railroad.

With my newfound pedal-powered mobility, however, I was able to explore both the IC and North Western yards on the south side. IC kept its 0-6-0 on an ash pit next to a coal conveyor south of the Seventh Street crossing, and there was a big wooden water tank on the main line just north of the freight house. The C&NW main line crossed above the IC on a bridge that pinched the latter's yard to two tracks, creating the north yard and south yard. The Seventh Street grade crossing cut through the middle of the north yard, where most of the switching was done; the south yard was used mostly for storage.

The centerpiece of the Dixon yard was the "puzzle switch," a double-slip switch that linked the House Track and the Middle Track with the "Wye," which was a connecting lead that climbed southwest from Seventh Street to the C&NW main line just west of the latter's passenger depot. (Of course, it wasn't until many years later that I learned the names for all of those tracks, or even realized that tracks had names.)

The North Western had a few sidings along its main line but lacked any formal yard. North Western's "Dixon Job" originated six miles west at Nelson, where there was a good-sized yard and roundhouse to serve the north end of the Southern Illinois line (the "SI") to Peoria and St. Louis.

The two railroads shared a five-mile joint switching line in Dixon. Built by the North Western in 1882, the "River Track" was equally owned, maintained and operated by both railroads (although it was always equipped with C&NW switch locks). The line curved north from the IC-C&NW Wye Track and dropped down a 3 percent grade to the river and then followed it under the IC, through about a mile of running in the pavement of River Street and out to the Medusa Portland Cement plant east of town.

Although it was sometimes called the "Sandusky," after the original builder of the cement plant, which was opened in 1906, the River Track was generally referred to by both IC and C&NW crews as the "Town Track." It had several local customers and two big industries:

the Medusa Cement facility and the Illinois Northern Utilities (INU) coal-fired electric-generating plant. In the 1950's, Medusa was shipping up to 40 loads of cement a day; meanwhile, INU received trainloads of coal in huge Chicago & Illinois Midland 70-ton gondolas.

Under the joint switching agreement, each railroad worked the Medusa plant on alternating days (IC on Mondays, Wednesdays and Fridays; C&NW on Tuesdays, Thursdays and Saturdays). And on the day one railroad would work Medusa, the other would handle INU and service the other Town Track industries.

The heavy cement trains, however, were more than one locomotive could handle, and the Town Track switch jobs were coordinated so that both locomotives would be available at the west end of River Street to doublehead the cement up the hill in the evening. Although the exact switching maneuver would be determined by which railroad was coming in from Medusa, they would always have the IC engine on the front up the hill.

By 1954, C&NW had assigned Fairbanks-Morse H10-44 diesel switcher 1082 to replace its resident 0-6-0, while the IC was still using steam. With the Medusa train strung out on River Street, the locomotives would line up at the Hunter Lumber siding at Peoria Avenue, directly across the river from Dixon High School. With the IC 0-6-0 leading tender-first and the FM diesel cut in between the IC caboose and the cement cars, they would whistle off and make a furious run for the hill. They would be doing about 30 m.p.h. as they rounded the curve between the INU plant and Freeman Shoe and hit the grade right at the First Street crossing—with the IC steamboat whistle clearing the way. By the time they reached Seventh Street, they would be down to a crawl, the 0-6-0 struggling with every exhaust and the FM smothering the neighborhood in blue smoke.

At the top of the hill, along the C&NW main line, the two jobs would split up, with the IC easing its cars (which were always lined up at the front of the train) down the Wye Track, across Seventh Street again and into the yard. The northbound and southbound cars would be sorted out and spotted for pick-up, and the IC Dixon Job would tie up for the night. Meanwhile, the C&NW would run around its train, pull out onto the main line and hotfoot it for Nelson.

Since the doubleheaders ran almost exclusively at night, I was never able to photograph one. But when they went up the hill, you could

hear it all over town. I spent many a summer night listening from my bedroom to that fight for the hill just before falling off to sleep.

It was about this time that Chet and I came to know the IC switch crew. Conductor Terry McGaw was a gruff old bird, and we tried to stay away from him, but engineer Frank "Ike" Eisenrich was friendly and would occasionally let us into the cab of the 0-6-0—although he never let us ride while it was moving.

One day, late in the summer of 1954, I had ridden my bike over to the IC yard and was exploring the south yard when I was approached by a man who turned out to be an IC special agent. That railroad cop read me the riot act and escorted me back to Seventh Street—just as a southbound 2-10-2 rolled into the yard, and I couldn't stop to watch it or even note its number. Letters from the railroad to my parents and grade-school principal got me into more hot water and scared me away from the yard for the next couple of years. Thus, I watched the end of steam from my dining-room window instead of the Seventh Street crossing.

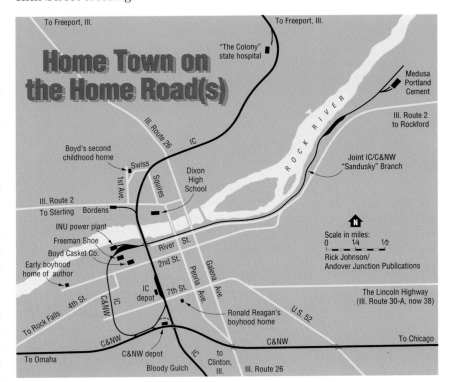

The End of Steam

Our steam show came to an end on January 17, 1955. Less than two years after they first began to show up, the black Geeps had displaced steam on the Gruber, with the Dixon switcher being the last to go (although we later learned that the Bloomington switcher

out of Clinton was handled by Mikados 1518, 1520 and 1521 until spring 1956). The 275 was replaced by a GP9, and from then on, except for one SW7, the Dixon Job was handled by Geeps. Since the Geeps were rotated to Freeport for fuel and servicing, a variety of engine numbers began to show up on the Dixon Job.

On April 1, 1955, I got my last look at IC steam in regular service. Chet and I went to visit his grandparents in Forrest, Illinois, and his Aunt Nelda in nearby Chatsworth. Although Forrest was on the Chicago-St. Louis main line of the Wabash—a route of handsome blue, gray and white F-units, E-units and Geeps—and on Toledo, Peoria & Western's east-west main with its olive, black and yellow Alcos, Chatsworth was on IC's Bloomington-Kankakee "Bloomer Line," which was still being handled by heavy 2-8-0's. Our encounter that day was with the 906, which stopped to work Chatsworth with the northbound local. When I returned to Dixon, I had to make my peace with the diesel.

Again, it was Chet who set me on the right path. "Just listen to them," he would say. "Those Geeps make a neat sound, especially when they are accelerating and have to throttle down to make transition and then rev back up again."

It wasn't the sound of a Mikado charging for the hill, but I had to admit that he was right, and on a heavy northbound train a set of Geeps would make a great chorus as they roared across the bridge and then "made transition" right outside my dining-room window. I've loved the sound of EMD 567's ever since.

I entered high school in the fall of 1955 and quickly discovered that Lloyd Swan's math classroom had the school's best view of the IC river bridge—and an early afternoon math class would usually get you a good view of the Geep doing the Borden's work.

Since the Gruber was the most-direct route from the Iowa Division to Paducah Shops or the scrap yards at Granite City, Illinois, near St. Louis, a lot of dead steam was parading south in freight consists. On one particularly memorable day, a southbound freight stopped to work the yard and left his train strung out on the bridge. From math class I had a perfect view of no less than three dead 2800-class 2-10-2's—and, of course, Mr. Swan was aware of my distraction and made a point of calling on me for nearly every question.

The football coach had similar problems when we used the practice field right under the IC bridge. I hated football then and still do today, but that railroad bridge made my one year of high school football bearable.

On the front side of the high school, study halls 201 and 211 looked right across the river and provided a fine view of the Town Track just west of River Street. At that time there was a rather humorous disagreement going on between the IC and C&NW. The North Western insisted that the small timber trestle on the Town Track directly across from the high school was not strong enough to safely support a Geep (which is why they kept using their FM switcher), while the IC inspector declared the bridge perfectly fit, and the IC never had second thoughts about assigning a Geep to Dixon. So in the spring of 1956, C&NW brought in a steam pile driver and a green-and-black F-unit and put on a great two-week show pounding the living daylights out of that trestle—all within perfect view of the study halls, which had their windows open in the warm weather. When the pile driver went away, so did the Fairbanks-Morse switcher, and C&NW joined the Geep brigade on the Dixon Job and even went so far as to assign an occasional SD7 (to my eternal regret, I never photographed that FM switcher in Dixon).

The fear of that railroad cop had by now faded, and I began to hang around the IC yard again. The grumpy Terry McGaw had retired as conductor and was replaced by Louie Scott, one of the most pleasant railroaders I've ever known. Brakeman Leroy "Govie" Bates just tolerated us and kept to himself, but the recently hired Jack Taylor didn't seem to mind our company. From then on we got plenty of rides in Louie's bright red transfer caboose.

It was sometime during my high school years that I got my first hands-on experience with railroading. My dad was sales manager for the Boyd Casket Company, which was owned by his father's brother, Arthur Boyd, and I spent a couple of summers working as a helper on the delivery truck and doing odd jobs around the factory. It was located on First Street about a block off the Town Track, and although it had no direct rail connection, the casket factory would occasionally receive a boxcar load of lumber which would be spotted on a siding next to the Freeman Shoe building. We would take the old 1948 Dodge flatbed truck to shuttle the lumber from the boxcar to the factory, only a couple hundred yards away.

Unloading a boxcar of lumber in the summertime is a hot, dirty and tedious job, as the

LOUIE SCOTT was the conductor on the Dixon Job in 1955 (above). The last IC steam engine author Boyd saw in regular service was 2-8-0 No. 906 at Chatsworth on the Bloomington-Kankakee local on April 1, 1955. Bruce Meyer had caught the 906 (below) on the same job in 1954 headed north from Bloomington.—BRUCE R. MEYER

PASSENGER GEEP 9210 was working the Dixon job in June 1960 as it idled on the North House track with a short consist including the resident transfer caboose. The operator's office was just inside the extended door shelter on the south side of the building.

long boards, piled nearly to the top of the car, have to be see-sawed out the side door. On one occasion my railfan knowledge saved us a lot of work when I noticed that the car was an old 50-foot automobile boxcar—with an end door. The boss of the crew didn't believe me at first; he knew good and well that boxcars don't have end doors. Then I swung the latch, and the end magically opened up with two doors. He backed the truck up to the end, and we made quick work of the unloading since we could pull the lumber straight out. I'll bet he's wondering to this day how many end-door opportunities he missed because he didn't know to look for them.

Expanding Horizons

As with most teenagers, my world began to expand, and through magazines and meeting new people, I was learning more and more about other railroads and railroaders. For example, I had become a regular operator on the big HO model railroad owned by C&NW engineer Don Goshert, and we were often visited by other railroaders and modelers. Aside from a few obvious railfans like Don, however, I was also rather disappointed to discover that most railroaders didn't like trains—to them it was just a job, and they'd rather be drinking or fishing or watching football.

I had been aware for some time that ex-C&NW 0-6-0 switchers were still being used at the Northwestern Steel & Wire mill in nearby Sterling, and I was constantly pestering my folks into taking me over there to see the live switch engines and the scrap line of dead steam locomotives that would yield such wonders as New York Central Hudsons, a Milwaukee Road 2-6-2, lots of C&NW Mikes and Pacifics and even a few IC 2-8-2's, including the 3969.

But it was through the magazines that I learned about steam fantrips being run out of Chicago and made my first one on the Baltimore & Ohio Chicago Terminal behind B&O 2-8-2 No. 315 on August 11, 1957. The ticket cost $5, and I rode to and from Chicago on the regular C&NW passenger trains. That trip got me on the Railroad Club of Chicago mailing list, and I was quickly plugged into the numerous Illini Railroad Club fantrips that were beginning to develop on the Chicago, Burlington & Quincy: 4-6-4 3003 to Galesburg, Illinois, on September 1 and 4-8-4 5631 and 2-8-2 5090 to Savanna, Illinois, on October 6, 1957, and in July 1958 a trip to Duluth, Minnesota, for a Duluth, Missabe & Iron Range 2-8-8-4. I learned that even though it was gone from Dixon, steam was not yet dead everywhere.

Incidentally, until this time I'd never been serious about taking pictures of trains, although I'd tried a few snapshots with an old Baby Brownie camera and then a Brownie Hawkeye, with results that ranged from horrid to almost acceptable. I finally talked my dad out of his Zeiss Ikon folding camera that used 120 film in a vertical format. It was a fully manual camera, but since I knew absolutely nothing about f-stops, shutter speeds or even focus, the results were completely unpredictable, though the camera was capable of reasonably good images if was set properly. I shot only black & white film, but in 1958 I bought a used Revere 8mm movie camera for the steam fantrips and began shooting ASA 10 Kodachrome.

To most kids, high school means just one thing: a car. And since Chet was two years older than I was, he "got wheels" in 1958—Robbie Benson's none-too-reliable blue '51 Plymouth. I browbeat him unmercifully until he finally agreed to risk that car on a trip out to explore some of the northern Illinois railroading we'd heard about—and maybe even find some steam.

Our first foray was a one-day venture downstate to IC's Minonk-Kankakee branch where we'd heard that a 2-8-0 might still be running. Instead, we caught GP9 9134 on the job. But in Kankakee we found a roundhouse full of dead steam engines, including 2-8-2's 1563 and 1655, Bloomer Line veteran 2-8-0 908, 0-8-0's 3503 and 3514 and low-drivered 4-6-2 2034. It was also my first look at *Panama*-scheme E-units on the main line, and we wrapped up the day at Joliet with Rock Island F-units, E-units, Geeps and RS3's and Santa Fe Alco PA's on the *Texas Chief*. The movies came out great.

The mobility of the teenage years opened up all sorts of new experiences, and it was about this time that I discovered what would become a lifelong vice: pizza! Al & Leda's Pizza opened up in 1960 at the foot of Fourth Avenue within sight of the Borden plant yard tracks—and the IC crew would often eat lunch there. They served the best pizza I've ever had (and do to this day at their new location down the street), and railfanning and pizza and Pepsi became a way of life.

While I had realized for quite a while that there was more to railroading than the Illinois Central, I was also becoming aware that there was more to the IC than just the Gruber outside my dining-room window.

In the spring of 1959 I graduated from high school, and my graduation present was a week-long steam fantrip to Colorado featuring CB&Q O5b 4-8-4's 5632 and 5626, Rio Grande F-units over La Veta Pass to Antonito, and three days on the narrow gauge to Durango and Silverton. The trip included a 130-mile cab ride in the 5626 at 75 m.p.h., doubleheaded Mikes over Cumbres Pass and a 2-8-2 working on the Colorado & Southern (that C&S 803 would be the last Class I steam I would ever see in regular service).

But more importantly, I was meeting other railfans, and that would pay big dividends over the next few years.

Champaign Tastes

In September 1959 I enrolled at the University of Illinois in Champaign—126.4 fast miles

THE IC YARD at Champaign, Illinois, still had a coaling tower and a collection of stored steam locomotives in the autumn of 1959, and steam had been dead less than a year. Mikado 1563 had been moved down from Kankakee, but the two 0-8-0's in the distance had been Champaign residents.

south of Chicago's Central Station. During fraternity Pledge Week, I discovered the interlocking tower where the Peoria & Eastern (New York Central), Wabash and Illinois Terminal crossed the IC main line and noticed a cluster of dead steam locomotives and a huge wooden coaling tower out by the roundhouse. That line of dead engines was made up of the two Mikes, 2-8-0 and 4-6-2 that had been in Kankakee in 1958 along with Mikados 1668 and 1691 and Champaign's resident 0-8-0's, 3509, 3541 and 3554, which had been under steam until early 1959.

The dormitory windows atop the Kappa Delta Rho fraternity house had a splendid view of the IC main line less than two blocks away. I claimed an upper bunk with a view out one of the windows, and on days when I didn't have early classes, I would awaken to the sound of E-units widening out on a southbound *City of New Orleans* or *City of Miami*, which would glide by in dazzling splendor in the mid-morning light—a sight and sound show unmatched this side of steam.

DICK STAIR was the daytime operator at Champaign Tower. He was a railfan, and sooner or later nearly every railfan student at the University of Illinois would make his acquaintance and as a result be introduced to one another.

Probably the best thing about Champaign in the fall of 1959 was the daytime tower operator, Dick Stair, a railfan who knew most of the other railfans around the campus. It was through Dick that I met Bruce Meyer, J. Parker Lamb, Phil Weibler, "Rusty" Ball and Ted Rose. Bruce was an avid IC steam fan and a recent graduate who had gotten a job with the Electro-Motive Division of General Motors and would return to Champaign to spend weekends in Parker's darkroom printing photos. Bruce and Parker had photographed IC 4-8-2 2613 working on the main line out of Carbondale as recently as January of that year (page 20).

I finally got my crack at a live IC 4-8-2 when that same 2613 was leased to the Louisville & Nashville for its 100th Anniversary excursion between Louisville and Nashville on October 24, 1959. I hitched a ride to Louisville with Rusty Ball (later to gain recog-

nition as a photographer and book author under his proper name, Don Ball Jr.). The 2613 was everything I'd ever hoped that an IC Mountain would be: It had a razor sharp exhaust and a mellow steamboat whistle that would "crack" into a scream when the cord was yanked hard—and it put on a show on the 1.5 percent Muldraugh Hill that impressed even *Trains* Magazine Editor David P. Morgan, who was aboard that day.

Rusty Ball, who would never let common sense interfere with his enthusiasm, discovered that the front door of the baggage car was not locked and went through it to climb onto the top of 2613's tender. It was a great place to hear the locomotive working up the grade, but Rusty actually passed out unconscious when the 4-8-2 worked full throttle into a tunnel and he inhaled a bit too much smoke. Fortunately, he'd locked his arms around a grab iron and didn't fall off, and nobody from the train crew knew that it had happened. As a result, that door remained unlocked, and on the return trip I ventured onto the end sill and watched the descent of Muldraugh in the dark by peering down the right flank of the tender.

We shot the 2613 the next morning in IC's Louisville yard (page 24), but we had to get back to school and couldn't wait until Monday when it worked a manifest freight back to Paducah. In February 1960 the IC put about a half dozen big engines to work out of Paducah for a couple of weeks, but I didn't find out about it in time to get down there.

J. Parker Lamb was a graduate student doing work in hydrodynamics and was a railfan photographer already well known in *Trains* Magazine. He took me along on a couple of his local one-day railfan outings where we got the one of TP&W's two F-units on a freight near Chatsworth and chased IC E6 4001 north out of Tuscola at nearly 100 m.p.h. on the *Creole* (Parker's dramatic pan shot of the 4001 made TRAINS while my dramatic pan shot had a pole blurred across the middle of the cab). But Parker taught me about f-stops and shutter speeds and how to focus the Zeiss Ikon, and my photography made an immediate improvement. In the spring of 1960, I also signed on with the *Daily Illini* campus newspaper and began to get some serious instruction in photography.

In May 1960, I had to choose between the Illinois Central and the fraternity. Railfans Al Frese and Stan Geyer from Rockford, Illinois, invited me to join them on a trip to the

Text continued on page 22

Vintage Champaign

STEAM WAS STILL being used in the yard at Champaign, Illinois, in the autumn of 1958 when Bruce Meyer captured these images of 0-8-0 3541 at work. On September 28 (top left) it was on the turntable and on October 6 was backing past the coal chute (above) and switching the big grain elevators (left) on the west side of the yard. By early 1959, Champaign's three assigned 0-8-0's (3509, 3541 and 3554) had run their last and were shoved outside into the dead line which lasted into 1960.—BRUCE R. MEYER

Vintage Carbondale

IN JANUARY 1959 Parker Lamb and Bruce Meyer were graduate students at the University of Illinois when Bruce heard that IC was running some steam out of Carbondale. They piled into Parker's old Chevy and made a four-day trek south to find it. At Carbondale on January 26 they found 4-8-2 2613 under steam and ready to handle a Cairo Turn the next day. The big Paducah-built Mountain was just another IC steam engine at the time but would go on in the next couple of years to operate a number of fantrips and become the last IC locomotive under steam. On this cold night in Carbondale, however, it was all work and no show business.
—J. PARKER LAMB

MIKADO 1537 was working a Thebes Turn out of Carbondale when Bruce and Parker set up south of Murphysboro (left) for a photo on the Grand Tower line to Gale, near Thebes, Illinois. Parker recalls, "That low angle looked pretty treacherous, so I decided to let Bruce go down by the water while I stayed up top and included him in the photo." They also encountered 4-8-2 2527 on a mine run heading south out of Centralia (below left) and passing through Bois (below), which is the station for the small community of Du Bois. This was some of the last steam to run on the IC outside of the Kentucky Division, which had occasional fire-ups into February 1960.
—J. PARKER LAMB

THE CARBONDALE roundhouse in September 1960 held, among other things, this pair of stored serviceable 2-8-2's, the 1610 and an unidentified sister. A pair of 2-10-2's and two Mikados were stored outside. Their next call to duty would never come, although steam had been used out of Paducah only a few months before.

Holy Grail of the Main Line of Mid-America: the steam shop at Paducah. Unfortunately, it was the weekend before final exams, and the Powers That Be in Kappa Delta Rho told me that I couldn't go—I went, and that was the end of my fraternity career.

Our first stop was Carbondale, Illinois, where the roundhouse was full of dead but serviceable steam. Inside were Mikes, and on the turntable radial tracks outside were two Mikes and 2-10-2 2747—at last, I could study an IC 2-10-2 close-up.

There was more in Paducah. Much more. The roundhouse was full of big stuff—2500- and 2600-class 4-8-2's and 2700- and 2800- class 2-10-2's—and outside were lines of just about everything I had ever dreamed of ex-

cept big passenger 4-6-2's and the rare 2-8-4's. But in the long dead lines there were 2-8-0's, 2-8-2's, 2-10-0's, 4-8-2's, 2-10-2's, low-drivered 4-6-2's, switchers and even a 2-6-0. There was nothing live, but the engines in the roundhouse were obviously serviceable and ready to go. Unfortunately, except for the 2613, none would ever get the call for service, revenue or otherwise.

When I returned to Champaign for the fall semester in 1960 (moving into a private residence hall, the only thing I missed about the fraternity was the view of the tracks) I used some of my summer earnings to buy a good camera from Parker. That 2¼-square rangefinder Kodak Chevron was one of his veterans, "It's the only camera in the country that you can run a roll of film through and don't even have to open the shutter to get trains on the negative," he joked.

And I got a chance to try it out in late September when Bruce Bailey, Ted Rose and I all jammed into Bruce Meyer's Volkswagen beetle for a trip to Carbondale and Paducah and a fantrip in Kentucky with the 2613. This time I had a good camera, a tripod and expert company, and the resulting photos have become personal classics: Mikes in the Carbondale roundhouse in the daytime and Mountains, 2-10-2's in the Paducah roundhouse at night and the 2613 in action.

We spent an entire day climbing over and photographing the lines of dead engines at Paducah, and I photographed Ted Rose sketching Mikado 1518 (Ted would go on to gain fame as a watercolor artist, while the 1518 would be the only IC 2-8-2 to survive, remaining in a Paducah park).

The next day, October 2, we went to West Yard in Madisonville, Ky., to catch the 2613 westbound from Louisville to Dawson Springs, Ky., with a fantrip. Again, the good camera paid off handsomely. I got my last look at her hammering the L&N diamond at Nortonville, making track speed for Central City. It was the last look any of us would get at an IC road engine under steam.

TWO TRIPS to Paducah in 1960 yielded countless images of steam stored serviceable in the roundhouse and in the nearby dead lines. In September, the low-drivered rebuilt 4-6-2 No. 2099 (left center) **made an interesting night photo, even though it was in the dead line and was missing its eccentric rods. The 2521 and 2507** (below) **were typical of the numerous 4-8-2's stored outside the Paducah shop, displaced by Geeps like the one idling behind them.**

ARTIST TED ROSE was sketching 2-8-2 1518 in the dead line in September 1960. The 1518 would be the only Illinois Central Mikado to survive.

Back to Reality

With the possibility of future IC steam all but gone, I went back to the world of black Geeps and orange-and-brown E-units. Champaign was a great place to watch trains, especially from Dick Stair's interlocking tower. Coal trains out of Kentucky would rumble endlessly northward with two GP9's on a hundred-and-some 50-ton twin hoppers with a red caboose on the rear. Hotshot manifests and reefer trains might get three Geeps.

Of course, the Peoria & Eastern, which crossed at the tower, was an interesting counterpoint to the IC. P&E ran its high-nosed lightning-striped black Geeps "Eastern style"—that is, long-hood forward—while the IC ran 'em as God intended with the short hood forward. Provincial prejudice is learned early, but it helps when you're right—you never saw 'em chop the long hood of a Geep for better forward visibility, did you?

The Illinois Terminal and Wabash were elusive players in Champaign. Wabash had a Geep-powered local that occasionally rambled

MOUNTAIN 2613 became a celebrity when on October 24, 1959, it was loaned to the L&N for a 100th anniversary excursion between Louisville and Nashville. On the following Monday morning it was under steam at IC's Louisville engine terminal (opposite page, bottom)**, preparing to work a freight back to Paducah. On October 2, 1960, the 2613 was westbound** (opposite top) **at West Yard, Madisonville, Kentucky, with an IC excursion from Louisville to Dawson Springs and back. Meanwhile, back in Champaign, the rail activity centered around the tower, where typical action consisted of a pair of black Geeps on 100-car coal trains** (two photos below)**. It took some patience one evening** (left) **to get the headlight streaks of trains passing on all three sides of Champaign Tower. Included in this northward view are westbounds on the Illinois Terminal (south side) and Peoria & Eastern (north side) and a southbound on the IC main (west side).**

25

UNIVERSITY OF ILLINOIS homecoming football games always brought in special trains on the IC. Here in 1960, four trains were lined up at the power plant near the UofI stadium with E-units up along the main line and a set of Geeps down on the power-plant tracks. The tail sign identified one train of heavyweights (bottom right) as having come up from St. Louis.

into town on the branch up from Sidney (12 miles to the southeast on Wabash's Kansas City-Detroit main line), and IT tended to run mostly at night with a local powered by an SW1200 on Flexi-Coil trucks. In the small IT yard west of the tower, Maury Klebolt's Illini Railroad Club had stored a cache of IT interurban cars as well as the heavyweight Pullman obs, *Inglehome*, which was being painted UofI blue and orange as the soon-to-be-famous fantripper *Chief Illini*.

But *the* show in Champaign was the passenger parade. Trains carrying heavyweight cars—both unrebuilt and modernized—as well as streamliners wore the splendid orange and chocolate, and nearly every train was powered by E-units on a main line legendary for 100-m.p.h. running.

Champaign was very much a college town, and the IC reflected that. On the days before and after holidays, the railroad would run "student specials"—passenger "Extras" comprised of a pair of E-units and heavyweight coaches that would run express from Champaign to the Chicago suburbs. They were usually rolling beer parties at the "century" mark.

Another distinctly UofI tradition were the annual football specials, where as many as three or four trains would converge on Champaign from north and south and unload on the main line and the sidings adjacent to the stadium on the south side of the campus. In October 1960 I photographed football specials with Geeps and E-units, including one that had come north from off the Wabash at Tolono a few miles south of Champaign.

And, of course, there was the old story about the passenger who was riding north on the IC main line. He asked the conductor, "What's the next stop?"

"Arcola," he replied.

"And the next?"

"Tuscola."

"Oh, sure," the passenger shot back, "and I'll bet the next one is Coca-Cola!"

"Nope. Champaign."

Eight and 52

A particularly impressive scenario took place in Champaign in late afternoon on every other day. Number 8, the head-end-heavy New Orleans-Chicago *Creole*, would struggle into the depot about 4:20 and begin the long process of loading mail and express. About 15 minutes later, No. 52, the every-other-day streamliner *City of Miami*, would slide in from the south and pull up alongside No. 8. After a quick passenger stop, 52 would whistle off and grandly accelerate out of the station, its mellow 12-cylinder 567 prime movers throttling back as it hammered the IT and P&E on either side of the tower and then swelling magnificently to "Run 8" for the hill up the main line to the north. A red Mars light on the boat-tail obs and a receding grade-crossing chime marked its passing.

And then No. 8 would come to life and re-peat the whole scene in an awesome encore. That's what the main line of the Main Line of Mid-America was all about.

Meanwhile, back in Dixon

By the spring of 1961, there was no hope that steam would ever return to the IC, but it was still very much a steam-era railroad with 50-ton hoppers, 40-foot boxcars, red cabooses and five-man crews. Standardized steam power had merely been replaced by even more standardized EMD power made up of E-units, switchers and *hordes* of high-nosed Geeps.

While I'd been chasing fantrips with the 2613 and struggling with engineering courses, Chet French was doing what he'd always wanted to do. In mid-July 1960 he had hired out as a brakeman on the IC at Freeport and was working east into Chicago, north on the Madison branch and south through Dixon to

THE ESSENCE of the IC in Dixon, Illinois, is summed up in this photo of a southbound freight with black Geeps on the Rock River trestle on October 3, 1963, with the stacks of the Commonwealth Edison power plant in the background.

A SOUTHBOUND afternoon freight made an impressive sight (top) from the small bluff above the Borden's spur on the north side of Dixon in June 1964. The train has just crossed the Palmyra Avenue bridge, and the Squires Avenue crossing is about 40 cars deep in the train; the box-cars above the Geeps could be viewed from the author's home. Looking toward the river (above), the units just passed over the Borden's switch.

Clinton. As a railroader, he was a natural. He kept the fact that he was a railfan pretty much low key and used his knowledge of base-ball to find common ground with the other railroaders. If somebody had asked one of his co-workers if Chet was a fan, they'd have like-ly replied, "You bet, a baseball fan!"

In January 1961 I left the University of Illi-nois and any potential engineering career be-hind. I hated math and physics, and my grade point average—or should I say lack of grade point average—showed it. I knocked around Dixon until the fall, when I enrolled in the photography course at the Layton School of Art in Milwaukee. I graduated two years later, returned to Dixon and immediately faced the fact that the world really didn't need one more trained but inexperienced photographer. I went to work as a darkroom hack for a local portrait studio. However, my education in pho-tography was put to productive use by docu-menting some of my hometown scenes in color using one of Parker Lamb's durable Kodak Chevrons. ◆

THE NORTH BANK of the Rock River from the Dixon High School to the area behind the Borden plant has long been well maintained as a public park, and in 1963 a family was fishing while the switch job wrapped up its work at the Borden plant and was heading over the bridge to the yard on the south side. The IC dropped downhill into Dixon and the Rock River valley from both directions, and the southbound trains had to climb the hill through "Bloody Gulch" (below), where Clinton-bound train 373 was seen behind the red sumac in the late summer of 1963 with two boiler-equipped passenger GP9's and a freight Geep.

CABOOSE 8006 was assigned to the Dixon switch job, and in 1965 it was photographed with GP9 9312 spotted on the Engine Track where the 0-6-0 had been kept. After Louie Scott retired and Jack Taylor became conductor on the Dixon Job, the caboose was often referred to somewhat irreverently as "Jack Taylor's Royal Red All-American Outhouse." Seventh Street is visible just behind the Geep. Every track had a name, and the four tracks behind the caboose are the South House, South Middle, Passing Track and Main Line.

THE "RIVER TRACK" to the Medusa Cement plant ventured down six blocks of River Street, where the 9090 (above) **was returning with Medusa loads in April 1970. One night in 1963** (right)**, IC GP9 9230 waited at Peoria Avenue and River Street to doublehead with the C&NW uphill with the cement.**

The Other Shows in Town

CHICAGO & NORTH WESTERN was Dixon's "other" railroad, and its Chicago-Nebraska main line always provided a good show. Four westbound Geeps (top right) **were dropping down Dixon Hill and crossing above the IC in April 1964, while the** *Kate Shelley 400* (above) **out of Chicago and bound for Clinton, Iowa, was arriving on an evening in 1970. Medusa Cement bought an ex-Nickel Plate Alco S2 in 1963 for its Dixon plant switcher, shown** (right) **in 1970.**

CHAPTER 2

Domain of the Diamond

ooner or later there comes a time when you should leave home for good, and for me it was in the fall of 1964 when I moved 42 miles northeast up the Rock River to Rockford and took a job as a floor assistant with television station WTVO, Channel 39, the NBC affiliate in the second-largest market in Illinois.

About a year later I moved into an apartment at 1125 Ninth Street, only a hundred feet from IC's Iowa Division main line at Buckbee Siding on the east side of town. The line had a half dozen freights and two passenger trains, the *Land O' Corn* and the *Hawkeye*, in each direction every day.

Rockford had a fascinating cluster of railroads just southwest of the downtown business district. The IC went east and west, climbing uphill in both directions from its Rock River bridge, and Chicago & North Western's West Chicago-Belvidere-Freeport branch paralleled the IC a few blocks to the north. Burlington's Rockford branch came up from its Twin Cities main line at Flagg Center, Illinois, while a Milwaukee Road secondary line came down from Janesville, Wisconsin, and continued south on the "Q" via trackage rights to Steward Junction to reach its own rails for the run on down to Oglesby and Ladd, near the Illinois River.

The IC, Burlington and North Western all had yards and engine facilities within sight of each other in Rockford. Both Q and North Western had roundhouses with turntables, while IC had a small metal enginehouse. In that concentrated area spanned by the Winnebago Street bridge you could find C&NW Geeps and Alco switchers, Milwaukee Road

Fairbanks-Morse switchers and hood units, Burlington Geeps and occasional "grayback" F-units and IC black Geeps and switchers and *Panama*-scheme E-units. Across the river, a network of industrial branch lines interlaced the southeast side of town with everybody getting into the action.

Completed in 1888 under the name of Chicago, Madison & Northern, the connection between Chicago and Freeport was one of the last main lines built by the IC, and in the 1960's it was a fast, heavy-duty single-track railroad with automatic block signals and train-order operation. Freights operated out of Congress Street Yard just north of Central Station on Chicago's downtown lakefront, and freight crews worked west to Wallace Yard in Freeport. From there the line continued westward to Dubuque, Waterloo and Council Bluffs, Iowa, with important branches to Albert Lea, Minnesota, Sioux City, Iowa, and Sioux Falls, South Dakota. The line, with some segments of Centralized Traffic Control west of Freeport, was famous for its "meat trains" of yellow and orange refrigerator cars bound for Chicago from the meat packers in Iowa and points west. In steam days, heavy 2-10-2's would hustle them over rolling topography of Iowa and the rugged hills of northwestern Illinois to Freeport, where 2400-class passenger 4-8-2's would sprint them the last 115 miles into Chicago.

In the mid-1960's, the *Hawkeye* was still a wonderful traditional hard-working overnight passenger train between Chicago and Sioux City, notable in that it carried a somewhat unusual something-for-everyone "6-6-4" Pullman

---

THE EASTBOUND *Land O' Corn,* **train 14, was breezing downhill beneath Cunningham Road approaching Rockford, Illinois, on a snowy February 1, 1965, led by E6 4001, one of only two such slant-nosed classics remaining on the IC.**

THE MEAT TRAINS that made the Iowa Division famous were still very much alive in 1965 as eastbound CC-6 (top) demonstrated as it rolled under the Winnebago Street bridge and along Kent Creek approaching the Rockford depot with a string of Wilson and Morrell freezers. Westbound CC-1 (above) at Ninth Street in Rockford that same year, however, was carrying the piggyback trailers that would soon replace the orange refrigerators. The image of an eastbound Geep on the main line at Buckbee siding (left) was framed in the window of Boyd's apartment at 1125 Ninth Street in 1965. And the only thing better than the view of a locomotive from your home is a view of your home from a locomotive, in this case (above left) from EMD prototype GP40 433A leading CC-1 in October 1969.

34

sleeper—six open sections, six roomettes and four double bedrooms. Westbound No. 11 hit Rockford at 9:35 p.m. while eastbound No. 12 was headed for the dawn at 5:30 a.m.

A more modern all-coach streamliner on a "shopper" schedule, No. 14, the eastbound *Land O' Corn*, complete with a cafe-lounge, originated at Waterloo at 6:45 a.m., paused at Rockford at 10:35 a.m. and arrived in Chicago at 12:15 p.m. Westbound No. 13 left Chicago at 5 p.m., hit Rockford 86 miles and two flag stops later at 6:30 and tied up in Waterloo by 10:55 p.m. With westbound schedules calling for 90 minutes running time to cover the 86 miles between Central Station and Rockford —including 15 miles of Chicago terminal trackage and two flagstops—those passenger trains were real hustlers. Until the *Land O' Corn* was downgraded in 1966, E-units were its normal power, while the two *Hawkeye* trainsets were regular recipients of IC's four high-geared (83 m.p.h.) GP9's, Nos. 9200-9203. Occasionally, it was vice versa, with the "Can O' Corn" getting Geeps and the *Hawkeye* a set of E-units.

It was a fast railroad for one with 60 m.p.h. freight and 79 m.p.h. passenger speed limits. One night I was at the Rockford depot talking

AUTUMN'S RUSTIC HUES surrounded the *Land O' Corn* as it dropped into Rockford in October 1964 with an E9 and E7 leading two Flexi-Vans, two baggage cars, three ex-Chicago & Eastern Illinois coaches and cafe-lounge 4151. The elegant profile of E6 4001 was displayed across Main Street (below) as No. 14 departed Rockford depot in June 1965. The fireman, entering the cab door, had just "keyed" the crossing gates.

with the engineer on the pair of E8's that had just brought the six-car *Land O' Corn* in on time. "What's the speed limit on this line?" I asked.

"Seventy-nine," he replied.

"Religiously observed?" I pressed.

"Of course."

"How fast were you going tonight?"

"About 108 between Colvin Park and Irene."

The fireman nodded in agreement.

Text continued on page 40

THREE OTHER RAILROADS shared the valley beneath Winnebago Street bridge in Rockford with the IC. In 1965 three Fairbanks-Morse H16-44's had Milwaukee Road train 367 (above) headed southward from Janesville, Wisconsin, to Ladd and Oglesby, Illinois, passing a Geep at the CB&Q roundhouse and a C&NW SW1 hiding in the trees by the white building in the background. In 1964, Burlington's 2-8-2 4960 was riding the Rockford turntable (right) beneath the Winnebago Street bridge during a fantrip out of Chicago that had come up the Milwaukee/CB&Q Rockford branch from Flagg Center, Illinois.

A PAIR OF E-UNITS in Run-8 lifting No. 14 uphill out of Rockford sounded as grand as they looked at Buckbee (above) on this brilliant summer morning in 1964. The baggage cars are on the Eleventh Street crossing, and Rockford Standard Furniture Company looms in the background. Eastbound local No. 92 (left) had GP7 8911—the same unit that was leading CC-1 on page 34—and two GP9's ready to depart Rockford after making a pick-up beneath the Winnebago Street bridge in October 1964 as the Rockford switcher made a move in the yard. IC's one-stall engine house was just out of the view to the right.

THE GOLDEN GLOW of the setting sun was reflecting off the four Geeps lifting an eastbound freight—probably a Chain Gang Extra—out of Rockford and up the three miles of steady 0.5 percent grade from Buckbee Siding. Boyd's vantage point was the Alpine Road overpass near the top of the grade.

Strange Bedfellows

For years, Central of Georgia had teamed with IC, Atlantic Coast Line and Florida East Coast on Chicago-Florida passenger operations. CofG contributed equipment to the *City of Miami* and *Seminole,* and two celebrities in this pool were CofG's only E8's, 811 and 812, delivered in 1950 in CofG's vibrant blue/gray/orange/black livery. While being regulars on the Florida trains, they were occasionally borrowed for other assignments, such as a turn west on the *Land O' Corn,* shown (below) Chicago-bound at the east end of Buckbee Siding in Rockford in 1956.—HOWARD PATRICK Following the Southern Railway takeover of CofG in 1962, instead of getting the SR black "tuxedo" livery like the rest of the CofG fleet, 811 and 812 were repainted into IC's *Panama* scheme, with CENTRAL OF GEORGIA lettering on the flanks and in the green diamond herald, as worn by 811 on the *Land O' Corn* at Rockford (right) in 1965. It was a time when families still came down to the depot to watch trains.

A DAMAGED BRIDGE on CB&Q's main line along the Mississippi River in August 1967 caused four days of detours over the IC between East Dubuque, Illinois, and Rockford. During one of those evenings, the eastbound *Afternoon Zephyr* (right) paused at IC's Rockford depot and shared the scene with the author's "motive power"—a green 1966 Volkswagen Beetle.

The Railroad Capital

**CHICAGO'S CEN-
TRAL STATION
was an impressive
structure at any
time, but at night
it created the
gothic image of a
fitting terminal for
Count Dracula's
Transylvania Rail-
road. The south-
bound _Louisiane_
awaits its 7:30 p.m.
departure for the
overnight trip to
Memphis and
scheduled late-af-
ternoon arrival in
New Orleans.**

My workday at the TV station was 3 p.m. to 11 p.m., which gave me mornings free, and I got lots of photos of the mid-morning east-bound _Land O' Corn_. The hilly descent on the west side of town was a favorite area with good photo potential and a couple of well-positioned block signals to tell me if anything was approaching. A typical daily routine for me was to have a Chili Mac lunch at the Loves Park Steak 'n' Shake and then drive to work by way of the IC tracks to check the signals. That pattern produced quite a few good action photos at varying times of the year.

I had known a few railfans from the Rockford area for many years, and through the Forest City Model Railroad Club I met a high-school student and fellow IC fan named Mike Schafer, who lived near the IC on the east side. Since I had a job and a car, and he had plenty of free time, we quickly teamed up for lots of one-day trips into Chicago or elsewhere to photograph trains. Other friends from Dixon and Rockford often joined us, and we really covered some ground.

Chicago, a little over an hour away on the Northwest Tollway, was the strongest attraction, and in "The Railroad Capital," the IC was just one of a couple dozen very interesting and colorful railroads. We soon got to know the gothic majesty of Central Station and how to sneak around in Markham Yard without getting rousted by railroad cops.

One of our favorite haunts was the 27th

THE ELEGANT slanted nose of E6 4001 stood out from the three E9's (top) at the 27th Street passenger roundhouse in Chicago in 1965. The 4001 had been there on October 14, 1963, with Soo Line GP9 2551 (left), which had brought the *Laker* from Superior, Wisconsin, into Chicago. To reach Central Station, Soo passenger runs used IC's Iowa Division from suburban Broadview, 13 miles out.

Street roundhouse, the "Home of the Stream-liners," where the passenger power was serviced and stored. During the middle of the day there was almost always an impressive line-up of E-units on the ready tracks, and occasionally you'd find maroon Geeps off Soo Line's *Laker* or New York Central E-units and Geeps off the Big Four passenger trains from Cincinnati and Indianapolis, which used the IC north from Kankakee to Central Station. Soo Line had in 1963 moved out of B&OCT's Grand Central Station and had begun running into IC's Central Station by way of the Iowa Division main line from suburban Broadview.

The ancient green multiple-unit cars that prowled the electrified tracks south of Central Station were a strange counterpoint to the freights and streamliners on the multi-track

A New York Central-IC power pool brought IC E7 4004 into Indianapolis (above) on NYC-IC's *Indianapolis Special* in 1965, where NYC's St. Louis-Cleveland *Southwestern* pulled in alongside. NYC used the IC between Central Station, Chicago, and Kankakee for its Big Four Route trains to and from Cincinnati and Indianapolis.

up to IC's white pinstripes and green diamonds—whereas Gulf, Mobile & Ohio's two-tone maroon E- and F-units or Burlington's classy Chinese red road-freight diesels were definitely tough competition. And anybody getting units with turbochargers and low noses made the IC look pretty old-fashioned.

The Iowa Division

The meat trains and manifests on the IC through Rockford carried symbols like CC-1 (Chicago-Council Bluffs), WC-2 (Waterloo-Chicago) and CC-6 (Council Bluffs-Chicago), and two of the freights were a bit unusual: eastbound AC-2 (Albert Lea-Chicago) and westbound CAC-5 (Chicago-Albert Lea/Council Bluffs). These actually carried hot traffic for connections in Minneapolis and St. Paul as a result of IC teaming up with the Minneapolis & St. Louis north from Albert Lea, Minnesota. Between Waterloo and M&StL's Cedar Lake Yard in Minneapolis, the IC would pool motive power with the "Louie."

The M&StL had been taken over by the C&NW in 1960, but the pool arrangement was retained, with yellow-and-green ex-M&StL Geeps replacing the red-and-white versions. I was never able to catch that pool train in action north of Waterloo, but I did encounter both IC and ex-M&StL power together at Albert Lea on the evening of August 5, 1964.

While I was taking night photos, a North Western assistant trainmaster came out to see what that bulb flashing was all about. After calmly warning me to be careful, he took quite an interest in my camera (one of Parker's

main line alongside, and we always found the orange South Shore Line interurban cars, which used the IC electrified line south to Kensington, much more interesting than the IC's own "wickerliners." It would be many years before we would fully appreciate what a superb and historic system IC's suburban electrification really was.

Chicago exposed us to nearly all of the great names in railroading, but having grown up with it, we always used the IC as a frame of reference. Few railroads' passenger trains could measure up to Illinois Central's fleet, but almost anybody could come up with freight power more interesting than IC's omnipresent black Geeps. For instance, I would consider the Pennsy's Alco FA's or EMD F-units more interesting, but in spite of their rooftop radio antennas, "P-Company's" wrong-end-forward Brunswick green Geeps could never measure

THE NOCTURNAL *Hawkeye* was a real steam-era passenger train that survived into the 1960's. The westbound *Hawkeye*, No. 11, was at Rockford (above) at dusk in the fall of 1965 doing a brisk head-end business, as evidenced by the postal truck at the curb and baggage wagons busy on the depot platform. In October 1965, two of IC's four "high-speed" Geeps, boiler-equipped and 83 m.p.h.-geared 9200-9203, had westbound No. 11 making its station stop at Freeport, Illinois, stopped just clear of the Stephenson Avenue crossing. At one time, IC shared the depot with C&NW Chicago-Freeport trains.

Chevrons), tripod and flashgun. When I set up to light the shot of M&StL 711 and IC 9161, he looked at that black Geep and observed, "When those IC guys are walking around a railroad yard at night, I don't know how the hell they keep from bumping into those things in the dark."

Symbol freight CAC-5 (which we called "Kack-5") was the Freeport District component of the Minneapolis-Albert Lea train, and it would rattle the windows of my Ninth Street apartment in Rockford in the post-midnight darkness. During the first couple of weeks I lived there, it would usually wake me up, but I always said that I'd gotten used to living by the tracks when I could sleep through CAC-5. My morning wake-up call was CC-1, the Chicago-Council Bluffs freight that rolled by in early daylight.

One of my most vivid memories of the IC in Iowa was something I didn't get on film. In 1964, No. 13, the *Land O' Corn*, would drop its cafe-lounge and coaches at Waterloo and sprint the mail cars 99 miles west to Fort Dodge. One night I was in the Rock Island interlocking tower at Iowa Falls listening to No. 13 coming at us shortly after midnight. The operator knew that 13 was a little late and

making up time, and he started comparing O.S. reports (station operators reporting its passing times to the dispatcher) with timetable mileposts. Thirteen was approaching Iowa Falls at well over 100 miles per hour! There was a long straightaway to the east, and soon we spotted the Mars light flashing in the sky. The two E-units slammed over the Rock Island diamond in a cloud of brakeshoe smoke as they tossed out the anchor for the 35 m.p.h. curve restriction in Iowa Falls.

I was duly impressed.

St. Louis and South

Illinois has two major rail centers, and each has its own unique character. Chicago, of course, is the greatest railroad town in the world, but greater St. Louis isn't far behind. And in 1964, East St. Louis had an irresistible attraction for any IC fan: It was home for IC's only Alco road-switchers, the three Alco RS2's which had been picked up with the absorption of the 18-mile Peabody Short Line in 1961. The 701, 702 and 703 were used in yard and transfer service out of East St. Louis. The nearby yard hump also was home of one of the IC's rare 1350-h.p. EMD TR1 cow-and-calf transfer units dating back to 1941.

St. Louis was also a particular attraction for me, since it had the highest concentration of Steak 'n' Shakes of any city in the world. But St. Louis was really about passenger trains, and while Chicago spread them out over a half-dozen big stations, St. Louis concentrated all of its trains into one big terminal. St. Louis Union Station was one of the grandest passenger facilities ever built, and the IC was right at home there. The orange and chocolate streamliners held their own against the crimson and gold of Frisco, the blue and gray of Wabash and Missouri Pacific and the red and maroon of GM&O and Rock Island, to say nothing of L&N blue, Pennsy tuscan and New York Central gray.

The station was ideal for photography with its sun-facing leads, multiple-track wyes and accessible road bridges over each throat. Every inbound train would pass beneath both bridges before backing into the stub-ended terminal with its immense arched trainshed. For outbound trains you had to choose one bridge or the other because trains would pull directly out of the station and turn either east or west to leave town. And when passenger trains weren't moving, gray Terminal Railroad Association of St. Louis (TRRA or, as we called it, "Trah-Rah") diesel switchers from almost every builder would scurry about grabbing onto everything from Pullmans to baggage cars to express reefers.

THE IC'S FIRST GP7 (right) **had a Gruber job southbound at Mendota, Illinois, on February 9, 1964. An IC southbound** (below) **was banging across the Wabash mainline diamonds at Wabic Tower in Decatur, Illinois, in July 1967.**

EAST ST. LOUIS was home to some unusual IC yard power. The TR1 hump set (above) **was one of only two such cow-and-calf sets built (IC 1350 and 1351); delivered in early 1941, they were essentially 1350-h.p. FT units in switcher carbodies. Also assigned to East St. Louis were the three Alco RS2's acquired with the Peabody Short Line in 1961. They were IC's only Alco road-switchers at that time and were used in yard and transfer service. The 702** (right) **was at the engine terminal in the summer of 1965.**

The IC was by this time down to only one offering in the hotly contested Chicago-St. Louis market, the daytime *Green Diamond* streamliner, which had been diesel-powered since the articulated trainset of the same name was introduced in 1936. But IC ran three trains in each direction between St. Louis and Carbondale, Illinois, where connec-

tions were made with mainline trains for New Orleans and Florida.

Mid-day in Carbondale in 1965 could be an amazing show of passenger trains. One brilliant spring day I was visiting Bruce Bailey, who was attending Southern Illinois University at the time, and we caught No. 101, the connection from St. Louis for the southbound

ST. LOUIS Union Station in 1965 was an incredible place to watch trains. On a hazy August day (above), No. 108-52, the connection from Carbondale for the *Creole* and *City of Miami* with E6 4001 in the lead, was backing into the terminal. All inbound trains backed into the depot.

ST. LOUIS BLUES included the B&O and Wabash (along with MP, T&P and L&N). Here in June 1965, B&O E6 1412 (above) had come in as the trailing unit on No. 11, the old *Metropolitan Special*. Wabash PA 1052 (above right) was outbound on No. 4, the legendary *Wabash Cannon Ball* to Detroit. Frisco's colorful *Meteor* (right) was arriving from Oklahoma City.

City of New Orleans, arriving shortly after noon behind E7 4007 and an E8.

Shortly thereafter, a pair of E7's slid in from the south with No. 8, the slightly tardy *Creole*. While 8 was doing its heavy head-end business, northward-facing E9 4039 backed in alongside and tied onto the consist of No. 108-52 for St. Louis. The 4004 and a sister E7 soon roared out of town with No. 8 and were replaced at the same mainline platform a few minutes later with an A-B-A set led by E9 4042 on northbound No. 52, the every-other-day *City of Miami*. After the through cars for St. Louis were cut out, 52 was reassembled,

A TYPICAL mid-day parade at Carbondale in the early spring of 1965 began with the arrival of the south-bound *City of New Orleans* connection, No. 101, from St. Louis (above) about 12:30 p.m. A pair of E7's arrived shortly there-after (right) with a slightly late No. 8, the northbound *Creole* from New Orleans, in the middle of its all-day run between Memphis and Chicago

During No. 8's long station stop, E9 4039 backed in and tied onto the consist of No. 108-52 to St. Louis (above left). Following No. 8's departure, No. 52, the *City of Miami*, pulled in on the same main track (left) along No. 108-52. With E9 4042 leading a perfect A-B-A diesel set on a matched consist, No. 52 departed Carbondale in grand IC style with its converted heavyweight boat-tail obs (above) bringing up the markers.

and soon its boat-tail obs was disappearing into the northern distance. A few minutes later, the 4039 came to life and moved out with 108-52, bound for St. Louis.

Our show wasn't over, however, for shortly after 108-52's departure, a Mars light from the north heralded the arrival of No. 1, the *City of New Orleans* behind an A-B-A set led by E8 4023. The huge streamliner dominated the station with its presence, just as the *City of Miami* had, but it was about to be upstaged. We had been fascinated by the little three-wheeled tow-motor that was scurrying baggage carts about and even took some action

ST. LOUIS-BOUND No. 108-52 departed as soon as the *City of Miami* cleared the station (top). **Another A-B-A set** (above) **heralded the arrival of No. 1, the *City of New Orleans*. The little three-wheeled tow-motor scurried the baggage wagons alongside No.1 until it "derailed"** (left).

49

pan photos of it—until it "derailed" by dropping one wheel off the station platform. As I said, Carbondale could be an interesting place.

The next day we were bound for St. Louis in Bruce's '62 Corvair. We paused eight miles west at Murphysboro under overcast skies and caught a somewhat late No. 101-53 out of St. Louis making its station stop in the city street. Westbound No. 108 out of Carbondale was waiting in a siding just east of town, and after 101-53 had cleared, it rolled westward up the street to the station. Seeing two passenger trains street-running in Murphysboro was an unexpected counterpoint to the multi-train interactions at Carbondale. All in all, it had been an impressive demonstration of major-league passenger operations.

Chops and turbos

By the mid 1960's, the IC was beginning to look pretty old-fashioned in light of the locomotive revolution that was taking place everywhere else. To notice the difference, all you had to do was go trackside at Dixon and watch the North Western breeze through town with

its new turbocharged and low-nosed GP30's and GP35's dating from 1963 and 1964, while the Gruber still saw nothing but high-nosed GP7's and GP9's. The only things that had changed about the black Geeps over the years were the repositioning of the bell from beneath the frame to an overhanging bracket on the high short hood and the "new" paint scheme, which consisted of widening the two-inch frame stripe to the full height of the frame.

But we knew that down on the Kentucky Division the IC was actually living in the modern age. After EMD had refused to sell IC any more GP9's when that model was discontinued in December 1959, the IC grudgingly went for 15 GP18's—high-nose, of course. It was three full years before the 9400-9414 were followed by IC's first low-nose Geeps, GP18's 9415-9428, in 1963. A few months later, in March 1964, the first of a dozen low-nosed GP28's (9429-9440) arrived. All of the new units were assigned to the Kentucky Division and were rarely seen elsewhere on the system.

In the first two months of 1966, however,

IN THE STREETS of Murphysboro, Illinois, No. 108 out of Carbondale had just met a late No. 101-53 south of town and is pulling in for its station stop in 1965. The depot is just across the street behind the photographer. IC had three trains in each direction between Carbondale and St. Louis, but one pair, No. 105 and No. 16, bypassed Murphysboro operating instead via Du Quoin.

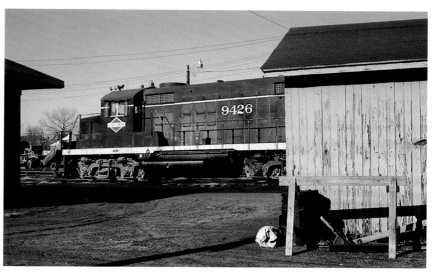

the IC finally became a truly "modern" railroad when it bought 40 low-nose and turbocharged GP40's. They were painted black in the "old" paint scheme with the narrow frame stripe and had no dynamic brakes (like every IC Geep before them), but at least they were the same GP40's that were setting the pace on nearly every major railroad from the New York Central to the Rio Grande. And the new, black GP40's weren't coalfield captives but masters of the main lines.

We Illinois Central fans could hold our heads proudly again. The domain of the green diamond now included the flanks of low-nosed and turbocharged diesel locomotives. ◆

THE IC BOUGHT 15 high-nose GP18's in 1959; 9406 was at Louisville (top left) in June 1965. IC's first low-noses came on the GP18's of 1963, like 9426 at Central City (top right). The GP18's were kept on the Kentucky Division. The low-nose tradition continued with the arrival in 1964 of a dozen 1800-h.p. non-turbocharged GP28's like 9437 (above) at Paducah on April 27, 1968. Turbochargers arrived on the GP40's of 1966. Although 3011 was at Paducah in 1966 (left), GP40's were used systemwide.

CHAPTER 3

An I-Ball to Eyeball

In mid-1966 the IC "Domain" went bonkers. On May 2, William B. Johnson replaced the venerable Wayne A. Johnston as president of the railroad—although the 68-year-old "WAJ" stayed around upstairs as chairman of the board. A man of quiet manner (some who worked with him even described him as "downright dull"), the 47-year-old William B. had just finished turning the hidebound Railway Express Agency into the much more modern and competitive "REA Express," and it was soon evident that he had similar plans for the stodgy Illinois Central.

Although a "conservative" railroad might be willing to sustain a $17-million-a-year loss on passenger trains, Bill Johnson wasn't about to, and he immediately applied to the ICC to economize the *Land O' Corn* and other trains and cut some of the local-service trains on the south end—surplus operations which were no longer needed. For now he'd stay away from WAJ's pride and joy *Panama Limited* and the *City of New Orleans*, but their day would come.

Under Wayne A. Johnston, the IC had seemed far more interested in preventing its neighbors and rivals from merging than in promoting any merger of its own. While its half-hearted talks with the Gulf, Mobile & Ohio were dying on the vine, IC was loudly protesting the Missouri Pacific takeover of Chicago & Eastern Illinois. The new man would take a much different approach.

Although Illinois Central Industries, the holding company that owned the railroad, had been around for some time, for all practical purposes it was just a name that showed up in financial circles and was invisible everywhere else.

Within the next few years, however, "Industries" would become a powerful force for massive and nearly disastrous change for the railroad. But before his first year in office was complete, the quiet William B. Johnson would dazzle employees, customers and railfans alike with a new Illinois Central Railroad that looked like it was ready to conquer the world—and you could have filled an Iowa Division meat train with slaughtered Sacred Cows.

Orange GE's!

The most sacred of those cows was the all-Geep freight power roster, and it was one of the first to go. In late 1966 IC announced that, in addition to 20 more GP40's, it was ordering six General Electric U30B's. It was the first non-EMD road power ordered by the IC since Paducah was building 4-8-2's (the Peabody Alco RS2's having been acquired by default). It was also a big step for GE, because the six IC units would be the first a.c./d.c. transmission units in the hands of a customer.

But the biggest surprise was yet to come. According to published reports, in late 1966 Bill Johnson had received authorization to spend over $50 million on 5,000 new freight cars, and looking out of his office window at Central Station, he observed that the freight equipment " . . . could look a lot better."

Illinois Central's Director of Public Relations & Advertising, Clifford Massoth, took on the task of creating a new corporate image with the help of art director Emil Cohen of the Geyer, Morey, Ballard advertis-

THE ULTIMATE EXPRESSION of Illinois Central's new 1966 image had to be the six huge Alco Century 636's acquired in May 1968. "Class engine" 1100 was at Mays Yard in New Orleans in August 1968. This was certainly no black Geep!

52

THE FIRST NON-EMD power purchased by the IC since Paducah was building steam was a half-dozen GE U30B's which arrived in March 1967. The 5002 was riding the turntable at the Markham roundhouse in July 1967. Incidentally, that steam locomotive is a Texas & New Orleans 1892 Cooke-built 4-6-0 owned by John Thompson, who was preparing to move it to his winery at Monee, Illinois, for display. The Markham roundhouse (below) held one third of the U30B fleet on this July 1967 day. The 5002 was moved into a stall beside its black brethren.

ing agency. After experimenting with variations on IC's traditional diamond, Cohen is credited with taking the most elemental image in railroading—the end section of a rail—and splitting it down the middle to create a stylized "i" and "c." The new symbol was a brilliant piece of graphic design. It could be reversed out in either black or white and remain identifiable whether used with or without its surrounding circle. Thus was born the "I-Ball."

But color was the kicker. They abandoned the traditional boxcar red for the rich intensity of burnt orange, a color that would work well with black-and-white accents. The paint was more expensive than oxide red, but the impact was worth it. Four boxcars were presented to the officers for approval, two in boxcar red with the new "I-Ball" herald and two in the orange. The rest, as they say, is history.

The boxcar colors were specified for delivery on the new GP40's and U30B's. Eager to see what the secret new locomotive image would look like, we began making the Indiana Harbor Belt interchange behind the EMD plant in LaGrange a regular stop on our weekend railfan ventures into Chicago. On a cold but sunny day in February 1967 we hit pay dirt as GP40 3046 was spotted close enough to the fence that it could be photographed.

The new GE's proved a bit more elusive when their delivery began a week or so later. It was quite a shock to see an IC General Electric unit on the Markham turntable. Every bone in my body told me that U-boats couldn't survive in a sea of Geeps and that the white carbody would be a terror to maintain, but I had to admit that the new image on a new unit in spring sunshine was definitely dazzling.

THE BURNT ORANGE color and "I-Ball" herald were first tried on two boxcars. The image selected was the one exhibited here (above) on a production car in a freight at Rockford. IC's first orange GP40's, Nos. 3040-3059, were shipped from EMD's LaGrange plant early in 1967. The following summer, a GP40 pair—orange 3050 and black 3023 (below)—had a St. Louis-bound freight rounding the wye at Gilman, Illinois.

Passenger Perversions

One of the things our imagination was running wild with when the orange and I-Ball were introduced was the fate of the *Panama* passenger scheme. Black Geeps turning orange were one thing, but the most-sacred cow in Mid-America was that IC passenger livery.

The first hint of change wasn't too bad: They simply used the block lettering on the side and replaced the passenger diamond on the nose with a black-and-white I-Ball. It wasn't exactly classic, but it wasn't bad.

THE *PANAMA* PASSENGER LIVERY did not adapt well to the new image. Although IC refrained from doing an E-unit in orange and white, it began by simply replacing the green diamond with the I-Ball, as shown on E8 4026 (above) on the *Seminole* at Birmingham, Alabama, on February 24, 1968 (that's Southern Railway 2-8-0 630 on the other track, about to depart on an excursion). Soon, however, came the "simplified" nose stripe as shown on units at Central Station (right) in September 1968—note that Central of Georgia 811 has no herald at all. Even as late at August 26, 1971, the I-Ball E-units looked pretty good as they handled the *City of New Orleans* (below) across the "temporary" bridge over the electrified main line at 23rd Street.

Then they had to mess it up. Trying to simplify the nose striping, they angled the side stripes into the nose-door headlight instead of sweeping them up the nose as God and the EMD Styling Section had intended. The end result looked pretty cheap, but at least they left the colors alone and didn't try to do an E-unit in white (it would take a few more years and a misbegotten merger to give us an idea of what an EMD covered wagon would look like in the orange and white [page 123]).

And even Alcos!

The new orange IC was not quite done with its tricks yet, however. Even though it now had chopped-nose units with turbochargers and even a half-dozen GE's, it was still ignoring the overwhelming trend for big six-motor units. That changed in December 1967 when IC took delivery from EMD of six 3000-h.p. SD40's (6000-6005) and five months later the first of ten General Electric U33C's. Now the IC had some real power.

Another sacred cow went down when the

PAST AND FUTURE were reflected in the pond at the Paducah engine terminal (above) **on April 27, 1968, as one of the new SD40's idled beside a veteran GP9. These first SD40's, 6000-6005, had no dynamic brakes. Meanwhile, inside the adjacent enginehouse, the first IC U33C, 5050** (below) **was being set up for its first revenue trip.**

ALCO CENTURY 636 No. 1100 was only four months old as it idled at Mays Yard in New Orleans (left) in August 1968. The IC had taken delivery of the six units (1100-1105) in April of that year. Three years later, in August 1971, the 1100 had lost most of its gloss as it sat in the Louisville engine terminal (below) in the same spot where 4-8-2 2613 had been under steam (page 24) on October 24, 1959. The same fuel storage tank provided an elevated photo platform for both occasions.

IC did the absolutely unthinkable: It bought six Alco Century 636's as its most-powerful diesels ever. Riding on Hi-Adhesion trucks, the big Alcos were an impressive sight when they arrived in May 1968. With their high horsepower, they got to stretch their legs on mainline manifests between Chicago and New Orleans before they were ultimately banished to the Kentucky Division coalfields.

In September 1968 I caught the almost-fac-tory-fresh 1100 at the Mays Yard engine terminal in New Orleans (page 53), but my all-time favorite encounter was with the same unit in the summer of 1971 at Louisville. In less-than-perfect paint, the 1100 was in the engine terminal sitting in the exact same spot where I'd seen my last live IC steam locomotive, 4-8-2 2613 on October 25, 1959, right after the L&N centennial trip to Nashville.

Text continued on page 66

The Orange Empire

THE NEW ORANGE LIV-ERY was very attractive when it was clean, as shown on GP9 9043 (above) at Hattiesburg, Mississippi, in July 1968 and on GP18 9418 at Louisville (left) in August 1971. Even in the 1970's, the GP18's tend-ed to stay on the Ken-tucky Division.

ONLY THE PAINT JOB was different as north-bound GP9 9145 hammered the Toledo, Peoria & Western diamond at Gilman, Illinois, in August 1969 (above)—the orange livery was being applied to older units as well as Paducah rebuilds. The scene at Gilman with the TP&W freight house and IC passenger depot was essentially unchanged since steam days.

HIGH NOSED GP9 9182 and Paducah rebuild 8072 led a freight through Memphis Central Station (above) in July 1969 with a consist of pulpwood racks that was typical of the south end of the IC but rarely seen north of the Ohio River. The passenger cars at the platform are consist for the *Mid-American*, the Chicago-Memphis remnant of the *Louisiane*. One of IC's earliest Geeps (left), GP7 8801 was a dual-control passenger unit often assigned to the Meridian-Shreveport mail trains 205/208 (page 68); it was in freight service with a U33C at Markham in August 1969.

The Orange Empire

AN UNUSUAL IC UNIT was GP9 9017 at Council Bluffs, Iowa, on a hazy July day in 1969 (right); it carried a chopped nose, but the 9000-series number indicated that it is not a Paducah rebuild. The low nose was probably the result of a wreck repair. The rarest of the rare on the modern IC roster was GP28 9441, shown (below) departing the Paducah yard in August 1968. The GP28 was EMD's lowest production Geep (only 26 units total were built, with IC 9429-9440 being the largest block, followed by ten high-nose passenger GP28's for Mexico), and the 9441 had been built as Mississippi Central 211 and painted IC black.

THE PADUCAH SHOPS had been used to rebuild IC power since steam days. In May 1967, Paducah out-shopped its first in-kind rebuild of an older diesel, SW7 200 (right), which had been built in 1950 as the 9300. One month later Paducah rolled out its first Geep rebuild, the 1955 GP9 9109 which became the rebuilt 8109, shown (below) at Freeport, Illinois, in 1968. The first few Geep rebuilds retained their high short hoods.

Paducah Geeps

By 1960 the IC had replaced 1,300 steam locomotives with 396 Geeps, 189 switchers and 46 E-units plus one GE 44-ton center-cab switcher bought in 1947 (and sold in 1961). The average working life of a first-generation diesel of that era was 12-15 years, and by the mid-1960's, a sizable block of IC's older units was beyond that 12-year threshold.

Back in the late 1950's, IC figured that two Geeps could handle almost anything on its essentially flat railroad, and manifests and coal trains alike rattled over the diamonds at Champaign with nothing more than a pair of black Geeps on the point. By the mid-1960's, bigger hoppers, piggybacks and more compet-itive schedules demanded more horsepower, which the new GP40's and U30B's would provide. But replacing all those older Geeps with high-horsepower units would be prohibitively expensive—besides, there were still a lot of jobs all across the system for which a 1750-h.p. Geep was perfectly suited. And although the Geeps were valuable as trade-ins on new units, since the IC was in constant need of more power it was even buying the new units without using any Geeps for trade-ins.

As it had done when facing the same dilemma of aging motive power in the steam era, IC turned to its own huge backshop in Paducah. By rebuilding and upgrading everything from switchers to 2-10-2's and even creating 20 brand new 4-8-2's, Paducah had revitalized the IC roster in the 1940's and postponed the need to dieselize by an entire decade—a circumstance which directly resulted in the Geep fleet that was now nearing the end of its economic lifespan. As had been the case with Mikes and Mountains, "Paducah" would be come the first name for Geeps.

Studies showed that Paducah had the capability to perform "in-kind" rebuilds of EMD units that would produce a like-new locomotive with a full 12-year lifespan for about half the cost of a new unit. In early 1967 Paducah tackled its first unit, SW7 No. 1200, which had been built in 1950 as the 9300. Although the horsepower remained unchanged at 1200, the switcher got new electrical gear and upgraded air-brake equipment. Although essentially unaltered in appearance, it emerged from rebuild in May 1967 in the new colors with a new number: 200.

The first Geep to get the treatment was the 9109, a LaGrange graduate of March 1955. In June 1967 it emerged from Paducah with much fanfare as the 8109 and burst through a banner reading "Better Than Ever." The statement was true, because the unit had been uprated from 1750 to 1850 h.p. and had gotten its crankshaft and cylinder liners chromed and remachined to new-unit specs, a new oil filtration system, new injectors, new protection devices, improved traction motors, new wiring and a modernized control system. About the only thing which hadn't changed was its appearance, which retained the high short hood. Dropping the number by 1000 would become the trademark of Paducah Geep rebuilds.

Four more high-nose Geeps and a few E-units and switchers emerged from the program in 1967 (the E-units were renumbered from the 4000's into completely new 2000-series numbers). In March 1968, a new characteristic of the Paducah rebuilds appeared on rebuilt GP7 7961: the chopped nose. The Paducah "chop job" involved removing a section of the sides between the lower portion which would remain and the bottom of the top edge roll. The roof would then be simply welded back on the cut-down sides to produce a low nose with a level top, rather than the sloping nose typical of factory-built low-nose GP9's, GP18's and GP20's. A two-piece windshield and full headlight and angled number board set completed the nose job. The 7961 also got two 48-inch cooling fans in place of the two

pairs of 36-inch fans, and the 1500-h.p. GP7 was upgraded to 1600 h.p. The overall effect was neat and businesslike.

Paducah cranked out a total of 14 rebuilt units in 1968, and by the end of the year it had a very efficient production line established, turning out rebuilt "GP8's" and "GP10's" from GP7's and GP9's.

In 1969 Paducah began adding the distinctive "frog-eye" headlights on the low nose in combination with rotating Pyle Gyralites between the number boards. Farr Dynavane/Dynacell inertial and paper air filters were added over the blower in an unusual "ox-yoke" housing atop the long hood. The internally simplified four-stack exhaust manifolds were applied, along with the newest 26L air-brake equipment, and the units were rewired to GP18 standards with new electrical cabinets. The 35 rebuilds of 1969 increased to 50 in 1970. "Paducah Geeps" were becoming a highly regarded industry standard for rebuilt locomotives.

"Old Mikes"

In the hometown of Paducah Shops, the only surviving Illinois Central Mikado is presently on display. Mike 1518 was rebuilt at Paducah before World War II and is typical of her hundreds of sisters. It is a very appropriate monument to the craftsmanship and dedication exhibited by the shop force of Paducah.

And while it would be nice to say that IC crews regarded the Paducah Geep rebuilds as highly as they regarded the steam rebuilds, that's not exactly the case. Since the railroad had no Alcos or Baldwins or cab units to com-

THE FLAT-TOPPED low nose became a Paducah characteristic after the 7961 in March 1968. Characteristics of later Paducah rebuilds were the "frog eyes" headlights on the low hood and a variety of housing boxes for paper air filters on the roof in front of the stacks, as shown here on the 8001 at Markham Yard on September 5, 1969. When Geeps were rebuilt at Paducah, their numbers were dropped by 1000, thus the 9001 would become the 8001.

pare them to, the GP7's and GP9's were the "lowest common denominator" in IC freight power. Chopped noses and shiny paint still didn't make them anything more than just a Geep—to most engineers—and after you've had your hands on a trio of GP40's, any non-turbocharged Geep is going to be a letdown. By their sheer numbers the Paducah Geeps would become "ordinary" to the crews, unloved but tolerated.

One night in the spring of 1971 an eastbound Extra out of Freeport, Illinois, was heading for Chicago and was put in the siding at Munger to meet CF-5, the "Bullet." (At one time the name meant all that it implied, but by 1971 CF-5 was the evening clean-up job that got all the westbound stragglers from Markham that needed to be classified at Freeport.)

The eastbound's engineer, Bill Reed, who looked more like a used-car salesman than a locomotive engineer, was on the radio to CF-5's engineer, E. O. Mayer. "E. O." was a jovial old-timer who wore the traditional cap and coveralls and usually looked like he was ready to go to work on a steam engine.

"How's it comin', E. O.?"

"Not so good," he replied. "We're just draggin' through Carol Stream."

"What've ya' got for power?"

"Just three of these old Mikes."

When CF-5's three Paducah Geeps finally growled their way over the hill and E. O. spotted the three GP40's on the Extra, he offered, "I'll swap ya' engines."

"No thanks," Bill came back.

So much for Paducah Geeps. ◆

THE PADUCAH SHOP program extended to E-units, but only a few were rebuilt. The 2024, shown (top) on No. 7, the *Illini*, at 18th Street on April 26, 1971, was originally E8 4032. Paducah Geeps were used everywhere; the 8004 (above) was at Cedar Rapids, Iowa, in October 1971—the IC seemed to be having trouble recognizing its buildings; that "freight station" looks an awful lot like a roundhouse! In October 1969, the 8072 was departing Markham Yard for Iowa (right) and was photographed from the Harvey YMCA.

WESTBOUND CF-5 was at AT&SF Junction approaching the 21st Street interlocking on June 27, 1971, with Paducah rebuild 8102 leading a high-nose mate. At the time, CF-5 was a relatively new Chicago-Fort Dodge train, operating more or less on the schedule of old CFS-3 (No. 73, the "Bullet") out of Chicago. CFS, meanwhile, had become a late-night departure out of Markham, replacing the once-hot CAC-5.

CHAPTER 4

Southbound Odyssey

Sometimes life takes a turn for the incredible. It happened to me in late August 1967. I was working at television station WTVO in Rockford, Illinois, when I got a phone call. "Mr. Boyd, this is Mr. Edwards with Electro-Motive in LaGrange, Illinois. Are you still interested in that job as a field instructor?"

I couldn't believe my ears. Back in 1959 at the University of Illinois I had met Bruce Meyer, who at that time was a "field instructor" for EMD. His job was to go out on the road and assist with the delivery of new diesel locomotives. A railfan's dream job if there ever was one. Dream on.

In July 1966 I had been taking night shots of Northern Pacific's first SD45's being delivered at Northtown Yard in Minneapolis and met another EMD field instructor, Bob Janicki. I asked him about the qualifications for the job and was surprised to hear that an engineering degree was not one of them. He told me how to apply for a job, which I did. A week or so later I got a letter from EMD politely stating that " . . . we're sorry, but we have no openings for anyone with your qualifications at this time." End of dream.

Until I got that phone call, I didn't realize how seriously they'd meant that bit about "at this time." In short order I interviewed for the EMD job, got hired, spent two weeks in the Training Center at LaGrange and suddenly found myself riding brand-new Great Northern SW1500's out of Minneapolis. For a 26-year-old railfan, it was almost too much to believe.

The field instructor's job consisted primarily of being a reporter: the Service Depart-

ment's eyes and ears out on the road. I had the entire technical resources of EMD at the other end of the telephone, and all I had to do was understand enough about diesel locomotives to observe what was going on and report it in understandable terms to the engineers and administrators back in LaGrange. Though the title "field instructor" dated back to the 1930's when the job really was to instruct steam-era railroaders in the whats and hows of diesel locomotive operation, in the late 1960's we were merely observers and specifically instructed not to try to teach maintenance or operation to the railroaders—that was a job for railroad officials, not EMD people.

Our job was to observe the delivery of new locomotives and report on their operation, primarily to be sure that the locomotives were properly set up and operating to assure proper performance and to protect EMD's interests in the event of future warranty claims. We would be on hand when the new locomotive was delivered cold to the railroad's shop and observe as it was given its pre-service inspection and start-up. The local EMD district engineer or a senior service instructor would usually supervise the shop work, while the field instructors would provide "rider coverage" by actually riding each new locomotive on its first road trip. We would then stay around and continue to ride until the last locomotive of the order had been given its 30-day "after service inspection." We would write a capsule Trip Report on each ride and note any problems the locomotives were having in a Weekly Activity Report filed with the Service Department. Getting paid to ride the

---

TRAVELING ENGINEER "PARKY" PARKMAN (white cap) and fireman Frank Brannan were chatting in front of manifest CN-5 on August 12, 1969, as they waited in the siding at Crenshaw, Mississippi, for a meet with northbound NC-6.

66

DOWN AT THE DEPOT in Sibley, Louisiana, on March 24, 1968, a passenger or two and a couple of railroad employees watched the arrival of IC train 205, the *Southwestern Limited*, bound from Meridian, Mississippi, to Shreveport, Louisiana. Number 205 would be discontinued in less than a week, on March 30.

cabs of locomotives and writing about it—this really had to be a dream.

But 'twas no dream. Dream job, yes; but not a dream. In 1967 I had assignments on the GN SW1500's and B&O GP38's and in early 1968 went on to the little Sandersville Railroad in Georgia with an SW1500 and then to the Cotton Belt in Pine Bluff, Arkansas, for a three-month-long delivery of SD45's, SD40's and SW1500's for Southern Pacific. During my time in Pine Bluff, I rode Cotton Belt SD45's into Texarkana, Shreveport and Memphis—and in the latter two, I checked out the IC whenever possible.

On one of my days off, Sunday, March 24, 1968, I drove down to Louisiana to explore the Louisiana & Northwest short line and IC's old Vicksburg, Shreveport & Pacific line through Gibsland, where I caught up with a living legend: passenger train No. 205.

The bolier Geep 9045, one coach and baggage car that made up westbound No. 205, the *Southwestern Limited*, made one round trip each day over the 313 miles between Meridian, Mississippi, and Shreveport, Louisiana. Not many years earlier, it had been the primary carrier of mail to the western parishes, but by 1968 it was obviously on its last legs. However, visiting stations complete with order boards and baggage wagons along its weed-grown but surprisingly fast single-track route was a delightful throwback to an earlier era.

Arriving at its western terminal, 205 would pull past and then back into the Shreveport Union Depot shortly after noon, usually shoving in alongside the colorful Kansas City Southern units on Nos. 9 and 15, the New Orleans and Port Arthur sections of the old *Flying Crow*. The IC Geep would then hurry off to get turned in time for its 3:30 p.m. departure eastward as No. 208, the *Northeastern Limited*.

These were the first IC passenger trains to be regularly assigned a Geep, when the two special dual-control, boiler-equipped GP7's (8800 and 8801) were assigned to them in 1951. The dual controls eliminated the need to turn the unit at each end of the run, but apparently the railroad later felt that it was cheaper to turn the units than to keep specific ones assigned there, hence the 9045. Unfortunately, this train was in its last week of service. After March 30, 1968, the Shreveport District would be freight only.

Other than the Cotton Belt, I didn't get

many assignments over the next year that put me in IC country, as I rambled around from the Georgia Railroad to Cleveland's River Terminal and the Western Maryland to the Milwaukee Road. One exception was an assignment with a pair of SW1500's on the Terminal Railway of the Alabama State Docks in Mobile in September 1968, which permitted a couple of weekend trips to New Orleans for a healthy dose of the IC's south end. In the summer of 1969, however, I got a most pleasant surprise.

Assignment: Illinois Central

When I reported back to the plant at La-Grange in early August after my vacation, I was delighted to find that my next assignment would be the Illinois Central, which was receiving ten GP40's (3060-3069) and 13 SD40A's (6006-6018).

I reported to our district engineer, Ed Formento, at IC's Markham roundhouse on Monday afternoon, August 11, where I received from IC diesel supervisor Bill Lamb cab permit No. 1299 (the same number as one of my best-remembered IC 2-8-2's). I didn't have much time to dawdle around Markham, however, because two fresh GP40's were being

prepped for service and would be out of Markham at 7:30 that evening on hotshot CN-5 to New Orleans. I was to ride them—out of Memphis! I was advised to hit the road.

All along my southbound odyssey, I shagged my butt through Kankakee and rolled along past houses, farms and fields . . . and made Memphis by 2 a.m. In the bright sunshine at 10:30 the next morning I was at Johnston Yard on the south side of Memphis, and CN-5 had just been called. The three-unit set that had come out of Markham the night before was ready to go: IC GP40 3060, black EMD GP40 433A and IC GP40 3062.

This was not your ordinary IC road set. The 433A was EMD's GP40 prototype, built in a modified GP35 carbody with SD45-style flared radiator housings (which were eliminated by using a longer carbody on production GP40's). And the two IC GP40's of the ten-unit Order No. 7171 were definitely not typically spartan IC locomotives. They had been purchased to become IC's contribution to an IC-Union Pacific motive-power pool through Omaha/Council Bluffs, and these units were deluxe versions with features re-

APPROACHING FROM the north, No. 205 saddled up to the west side of Shreveport Union Station. Once past the throat of the the stub-end terminal, it would back in from the south. The Kansas City Southern E7 and F7B had brought No. 9 down from Kansas City, and the KCS switcher was swapping cars between No. 9 to New Orleans and No. 15 to Port Arthur.

MANIFEST CN-5 (above) was ready to depart Johnston Yard in Memphis, Tennessee, on August 12, 1969, with brand-new GP40's 3060 and 3062 bracketing EMD's prototype GP40, the black-painted 433A. At the throttle out of Memphis (below) was engineer Mike Braddley, who would handle the train south along the Tallahatchie District to Gwin, Mississippi.

THE ENGINEER got this view (above) of CN-5 as he inspected his train at Philipp, Mississippi, on one of the few curves on the Tallahatchie District. This was the first dynamic-brake-equipped IC road set to run the Chicago-New Orleans main line, and traveling engineer Parkman demonstrated their use as the train approached the statutory stop at the Columbus & Greenville crossing in Greenwood.

quired by UP—most notably, they were the first units bought by IC to be equipped with dynamic brakes (and these were the newest extended-range dynamics). In addition they had the big L-shaped cab front window on the engineer's side and Gyralites. Since the 433A also had dynamics, the power on CN-5 at Memphis this day was the first completely dynamic-brake-equipped IC road set to run the main line.

The Illinois Central actually had two main lines between Memphis and Jackson, Mississippi, that paralleled each other about 25 miles apart. The Tallahatchie and Yazoo districts that I was about to ride on CN-5 made up the freight line, while the Grenada, Water Valley and Canton districts comprised the passenger main to the east. Although the single-track passenger main was straighter and faster (79 m.p.h.), it had a roller-coaster profile caused by the numerous streams feeding

into the Mississippi River flood plain. Those humpbacks made handling a freight over the line nearly impossible. The Tallahatchie-Yazoo freight line, on the other hand, stayed down in the flat flood plain but missed most of the big towns in the region. So the passenger trains ran the Grenada District and the freights ran the Tallahatchie.

In the cab of the 3060 as we departed Memphis were the engineer and fireman, a travelling engineer and myself (the head brakeman had gone back to ride the second unit). The engineer was a friendly middle-aged Irishman named Mike Braddley, while the fireman, Frank M. "Splinter" Brannan, was a cheerful old timer who looked like he should have been the engineer (Brannan was a promoted engineer who'd had a heart attack a couple of years earlier and was restricted to service as a fireman). Traveling engineer Elliott G. Parkman was a pleasant

AT CRENSHAW, Mississippi, CN-5 took the siding to meet northbound NC-6, powered by GP40 3012 and two SD40's. While CN-5's head brakeman watched from the other side, traveling engineer Parkman and fireman Brannan inspected NC-6 from the ground while engineer Braddley shouted a greeting from the cab window.

but businesslike young fellow dressed in coveralls and wearing a white cap with an IC green diamond on it—the classic image of a steam-era diesel man.

New Orleans-bound manifest CN-5 had 58 loads and 29 empties totaling 5,245 tons, a pretty-good-sized train. Traveling Engineer "Parky" Parkman had worked on the SP as well as some of the EMD SD45 demonstrator sets on the IC out of Centralia (Illinois) and knew quite a bit about *dynamic* brakes, and he and I were determined that the IC was going to start out right by calling them by their proper name—not "dah-a-matic brakes" like we'd heard a couple of the local mush-mouths in the engine terminal call them. Parky kept us fairly busy for the first dozen or so miles checking Mike out on the dynamics. Once Mike got comfortable with his new toy, things settled down to a placid routine.

As we rolled southward, I was standing behind Mike casually watching the ammeter and his throttle handling while Parky and Splinter occupied the two left-side seats. I overheard the fireman ask Parky if he'd "ever seen an 1100 with a Cole trailer truck?"

Hey, that sounded like steam talk! I paid closer attention as Splinter pulled an 8×10 photo from his bag and began to point out some details to Parky. It didn't take long for the three of us to realize that we were all

railfans who spoke the same language (Parky, it turns out, had scratchbuilt a model of an IC 2400-class 4-8-2 in HO scale and was an avid steam fan).

The businesslike reserve quickly vanished, and we spent the rest of the trip mixing lineside observations and operational notes with pure railfan chatter. The 155-mile Memphis-to-Gwin, Mississippi, Tallahatchie District was a fairly flat piece of single-track, 45-m.p.h. railroad burdened with a frustrating number of 25-m.p.h. slow orders. As for lineside features, we passed a classic Mississippi prison chain gang working on an adjacent road, and the crew pointed out the "Tallahatchie Bridge" that was prominently mentioned in the popular 1967 song "Ode to Billie Joe" by Bobbie Gentry.

While we were in the siding at Crenshaw to meet our northbound counterpart, NC-6, a one-Geep local scurried in and made a set-out on the house track before the manifest arrived behind a black GP40 and two of the low-6000 SD40's. The meet between IC's two hottest New Orleans manifests at a hand-thrown siding on a weedy single-track railroad was definitely not what I'd imagined the south end of the Main Line of Mid-America would look like.

Dropping down a slight grade to the statutory stop at the Columbus & Greenville diamond in Greenwood, Parky put on an impressive demonstration of mixing the extended-range dynamics with the automatic air brake to plant that train precisely at the stop board in the fastest and smoothest stop I'd ever experienced. (Extended-range dynamics are superior to conventional dynamics in that they retain their effectiveness down to a much lower speed, long after the slower motor rotation causes conventional dynamics to fade out.) That C&G crossing, incidentally, was guarded by a swinging gate whose normal position was defined in the timetable as "as last used," requiring the statutory stop.

Mike Braddley had been using the dynamics to good advantage for the entire trip and was having a ball with them. By the time he brought the train to a halt at the division point at Gwin, he was handling them like a veteran.

Parky had to get back to Memphis and hopped off at the crew change at Gwin to

catch a northbound. I would ride on down to Jackson to show the new crew the basics of dynamic brakes. As he left for the beanery with the Tallahatchie District crew, Parky told me that I'd be missing the best part of the trip: hearing Mike Braddley tell everybody who'd listen how he'd mastered "them dynamic brakes!"

Ridin' on the City of New Orleans

After the ride with Parky, the trip with CN-5's Yazoo District crew on down the 72 miles to Jackson was uneventful. I sacked out that night in a motel and was up the next morning, August 13, for the 10:15 a.m. arrival of the northbound *City of New Orleans*.

Number 2 wasn't much of a train from New Orleans north to Jackson; it arrived with three E-units, a baggage car and two coaches. A "Palm Grove Cafe" car, a club-

THE BIG DEPOT at Winona, Mississippi, was framed in the cab window of E8 4022 as IC No. 2, the northbound *City of New Orleans*, eased in for its passenger stop on August 13, 1969, where there were plenty of folks waiting to board the daytime streamliner for Memphis and other points north.

73

lounge, two "straight" coaches and a dome coach were added at Jackson. The motive power was the 4022 and a sister E8A bracketing E7A 4016. Wanting to sample breakfast in the diner and try the view from the dome, I opted to "ride the cushions" 58 miles up to Durant, Mississippi.

Ridin' on the *City of New Orleans*, Illinois Central *Wednesday* mornin' rails . . . and Friday the 13th came on Wednesday this month. It was going to be a strange but interesting trip. The French Toast *à la* IC in the diner was good if not spectacular, and I was just finishing up as we rolled uneventfully through Vaughan, Mississippi, where Casey Jones had gone to Glory back on April 30, 1900.

I spent the rest of the ride to Durant in the ex-Missouri Pacific Pullman-Standard dome coach. Its only two inhabitants were the flagman and myself, and the dome was a rather claustrophobic affair with its roof and center-end glass panels having been replaced with steel plating. The Burlington would never have permitted anything like that! By the time we got to Durant, I was ready for a

much better place to ride.

During the station stop at Durant, I went forward and introduced myself to the engineer, Jim Larson, showing him my cab pass. "From EMD, eh? Well, maybe you can help my fireman. He's in the back; one of the units isn't loading right."

In spite of the fact that I knew virtually nothing about the electrical system of an E8, I said that I'd give it a try. But as I stepped into the engine room right behind the 4022's cab, I noticed quite a lot of smoke. Then I noticed quite a bit of fire!

While it was a somewhat spectacular surprise, I immediately recognized that it was a relatively benign blaze in the "vee" at the top of the engine around the base of the exhaust manifolds. Crud and leaked oil can accumulate there and be ignited by heat or minor leaks in the manifold. It can be scary, but there really isn't anything in the immediate area that will spread the flames, and such a fire will usually just consume itself.

I immediately went back up to the cab and informed the engineer of the condition of his No. 1 prime mover. He hurried back to

AS A GAGGLE of passengers clambered to board the coaches of No. 2 pausing at Batesville, Mississippi, the fireman was climbing out of the electrically troubled third unit. A fire had already been put out atop the front engine of the lead locomotive.

74

PARKY PARKMAN was on hand as the *City of New Orleans* arrived at Memphis Central Station. For a view from Parky's office in the depot of the train ready to depart following its crew change, see page 2.

the engine room, grabbed the CO_2 fire extinguisher and handed it to *me*! I protested that I'd never handled one of those things, but then he said that *he* hadn't either and that he just figured that it should be the "factory man's" job.

I doused the smoky fire with a sooty white puff of CO_2. Just as the soot and smoke began to dissipate and things were airing out, the fireman showed up, the communicator whistle tweeted twice and we were ready to go.

The engineer skinned 'er back, and the old 567's roared to life. We were bound for Memphis with a vengeance. A couple of miles out of town we were hitting about 50 m.p.h., and I went back into the engine room to check on our fire, which should have been completely out. It was, however, merrily blazing away atop the thundering V-12. I hauled out the extinguisher and again thoroughly doused the fire.

Have you ever used a CO_2 fire extinguisher? It puts out a chalky white soot that gets all over everywhere—especially if the electrical cabinet doors leak and the engineer and fireman have the cab windows open in a 50-m.p.h. breeze! I ducked into the cab for some fresh air, only to discover that the windows had drawn the soot and smoke into the cab and the engineer and fireman were both hanging out of their respective side doors to breathe—and the train was being brought to a rapid halt. As the units stopped, we all hopped to the ground to get some fresh air.

The conductor was on the radio, mad as a hornet. "Hey, you can't stop here! We've got crossings blocked."

The engineer bellowed back, "Our damned engine's on fire. You wanna' bet we can't stop here?"

Things were quickly brought under control; the fire was completely out and the cab and engine room were airing out. We were soon moving again, and there was no more trouble with the fire from there on.

The stations at Winona, Grenada and Batesville all had loaded baggage wagons and respectable crowds of passengers waiting to board the *City*. Parky was standing on the platform in Memphis as we arrived, and after a couple of photos at track level, I went with him into his office high up in the station and got an impressive photo looking down onto the E-units as they prepared to depart (page 2). Parky took me out to his home where his wife had dinner ready, and I got a close look at that HO scale 2400 passenger Mountain.

I'd have been humming "City of New Orleans" all day, except that Steve Goodman hadn't written it yet.

UNION PACIFIC units in the North Platte-to-Chicago pool made it to New Orleans on August 14, 1969, where at Mays Yard (right) an IC GP40 was teamed with a UP GP30 booster and conventional GP30. Engine terminals in the Deep South were different from those up north. While Mays Yard had a spartan metal building, the old Gulf & Ship Island roundhouse (below) at Gulfport, Mississippi, was an open-air steam-era relic, shown in August 1968. A year later, Hurricane Camille destroyed the Gulfport roundhouse and "Charity Hilton" crew bunkhouse

Hurricane party

From Memphis I headed south for New Orleans, checking out my three-unit GP40 set returning north on NM-6 at 2 a.m. Thursday in Jackson before calling it a night. I continued to New Orleans later that day and went to Mays Yard for a line-up. I'd made two visits to New Orleans while assigned to Mobile in 1968, so I was reasonably familiar with the rail scene there. No new units were headed my way, so I had a couple of days to kill.

After being accustomed to the huge complex of Markham Yard in Chicago, Mays Yard has never ceased to amaze me, for its modest middle-of-a-wye engine facility and small yard are definitely not what I'd expected to find at the "other end" of the IC. The huge Stuyvesant Docks yard, where shiploads of bananas were once transferred into yellow refrigerator cars for the trip north, was nearly vacant by 1969. New Orleans, however, had other attractions. In the Mays engine terminal, for instance, tied to a black IC GP40 was a UP GP30 and UP GP30 cabless booster; the UP power pool for which the new GP40's had been ordered had been implemented since February.

On Friday, August 15, while checking in at Mays about my GP40's, I caught the inbound *Panama Limited* with an A-B-A set of E-units—and the two A-units were IC's only remaining E6's: 4001 and 4003! Taking advantage of the sunny day, I got some photos of them at the downtown New Orleans Union Passenger Terminal diesel shop and that afternoon drove some 40 miles north to Pass Manchac, where a stream connects Lake Ponchartrain and Lake Maurepas, and the IC has a 170-foot swing bridge with long timber trestle approaches. Viewed from the high span of the parallel U.S. 51 bridge, the northbound *Panama* made a beautiful sight in the late afternoon sunlight (pages 78-79).

On Saturday, GP40's 3065, 3064 and 3067 came in on CN-5 and went north that evening on NM-6. I rode the train up to McComb, Mississippi, and returned to New Orleans on MN-3 with the 3063, 3068 and 3066. Both were relatively uneventful trips and mostly in the dark, but they gave me a first-hand look at the IC's route through the bayous.

Sunday evening, August 17, 1969, however, would be quite different, because the news was reporting that Hurricane Camille was headed right for New Orleans. It hit the coast that night just east of the city, and I "rode it out" in my room at Rozal's Motel in Metairie. The motel owner had gotten a trucker to park his semi trailer in front of his lobby's big glass windows to protect them. The wind and rain were spectacular but did relatively little damage on our west side of town. The area between New Orleans and Mobile was not so fortunate, however.

Just before the hurricane hit, I had gotten orders from LaGrange to pack up and move to Birmingham, Alabama, to cover the SD40A's which would soon be arriving there. About mid-day Monday I ventured eastward up Highway 11 into the hurricane-ravaged countryside. There were a lot of downed trees and wires, and marine and property damage was very evident. As I was crossing the long bridge over the east end of Lake Ponchartrain toward Slidell, my green Volkswagen Squareback wagon let out a terrible ripping noise as the engine dropped a valve. Sounding like an out-of-tune machine gun, the en-

THE AUTHOR posed with his brand new Volkswagen Squareback beneath the Dixon IC trestle in February 1969. On August 18, this car dropped a valve and hammered 270 miles across hurricane-ravaged country with a blown engine.
—MIKE SCHAFER

gine kept running, and I pulled into the nearest motel after reaching dry land. Because of the people displaced from their homes by the hurricane damage, I was informed that there was not a motel room available for two hundred miles in any direction!

With no place to stay, I had no choice but to see just how long that VW would keep running. With the engine gradually tearing itself apart, I headed for Birmingham, losing another gear in the transmission about every 50 miles. I hammered—literally—across Mississippi on Route 11 and was well into Alabama by dark. By then the Squareback was running in second gear (the only one it had left), and the clutch was no longer working, so I couldn't risk stopping. Luckily I'd filled the

Text continued on page 80

THREE BRAND NEW GP40's arrived in New Orleans on CN-5 on August 16, 1969, and spent most of the day in the Mays engine terminal before returning north that evening on NM-6 (below), where the gloomy sky over Mays Yard was a precursor of Hurricane Camille, approaching over the Gulf and less than 24 hours away.

THE *PANAMA LIMITED* had lost its Pullman-only status by August 15, 1969, but it still made a grand sight northbound in late afternoon at Pass Manchac, Louisiana, 40 miles north of New Orleans. The swing bridge (right) spans the navigable channel between Lake Ponchartrain and Lake Maurepas. Power this day was a remarkable A-B-A set of E-units with IC's only surviving E6's bracketing an E8B. The IC's first E6, 4000, was purchased in October 1940 for the *City of Miami* and adorned in a unique green-and-orange "bow wave" livery. E6's 4001-4004 were delivered in November 1941 and introduced the striking orange-and-chocolate livery (designed by the EMD Styling Section) that became the IC standard. The four units were lettered for *Panama Limited* service, resulting in the orange and chocolate becoming known thereafter as the "*Panama* scheme." E6 4000 was rebuilt as E7 4000 in 1947 and renumbered 4004 following the retirement of E6 4004 in 1954. The E6 4002 was retired in 1961, leaving the 4001 and 4003 as the only slant-nosed survivors—but still worthy of assignments on the *Panama Limited*.

HALEYVILLE, in far northwest Alabama, is where IC's Birmingham District left home rails and entered 41 miles of Southern Railway trackage rights south to Jasper. In August 1969 a typical Geep set had hotshot SE-1 pausing there for a crew change.

tank while the clutch was still functional, and a VW gets great gas mileage, even in second gear. The air-cooled four finally lurched and gasped its last right in front of football coach Paul "Bear" Bryant's VW dealership in Tuscaloosa—within sight of the first motel I'd seen since New Orleans with a VACANCY sign lighted. The car had made 270 miles with a blown engine!

Next morning I left the VW in the care of the Bear, hopped Southern's *Southerner* to Birmingham at 1:31 p.m. and rented a car in the Steel City of the South. A week and $375 later, I got my VW back with a new engine, clutch and transmission.

Birmingham Train Control

The IC's route out of Jackson, Tennessee, into Birmingham is one of the most unusual on the system because it involves trackage rights over three other railroads. And since two of those railroads, the Southern and the Frisco, had their own type of Automatic Train Control—and each was different from the IC's—any locomotive in the lead on a Birmingham train had to be equipped with all three systems. On the IC this was known as "Birmingham Train Control," and locomotives

so equipped were kept assigned there. This, I discovered, is why I'd never before seen certain low-9000 series GP9's, for they were among the units specially equipped for Birmingham service. My new SD40A's were also equipped with Birmingham Train Control.

The Birmingham line was pieced together around 1908 while the IC was energetically expanding through the Deep South in response to the opening of the Panama Canal and the booming industrial potential in the area. The Birmingham line began at Jackson, Tennessee, which was on the freight line south out of Fulton, Kentucky. Just south of IC's Frogmoor Yard on the south side of Jackson, the Birmingham line entered Gulf, Mobile & Ohio track at Perry, Tennessee, which it used for 51 miles south to Ruslor Junction at Corinth, Mississippi. The IC then owned 80 miles of its own track from Corinth south to Haleyville, Alabama, where it picked up Southern Railway trackage rights for 41 miles to Jasper before turning left onto the Frisco for the last 36 miles into Birmingham.

The Birmingham District was part of the St. Louis Division, and the hottest trains on the railroad, southbound SE-1 and northbound BC-4 between Chicago and Birmingham, both had St. Louis connections at Fulton. In Birmingham, IC used East Thomas Yard on the northwest side of town. Although it looked like one big yard, it was actually two yards side by side, with the Frisco facility on the south side of the main line and the IC and Central of Georgia sharing the yard on the north side.

The 13 SD40A's of EMD Order 5743 were unique locomotives, as they were essentially 3000-h.p. SD40's built on five-foot-longer SDP45 frames to accommodate a 5,000-gallon fuel tank ("normal" SD40's have a 4,000-gallon tank). The 6005-6017 also had extended-range dynamic brakes, the L-shaped engineer's front windows and Gyralites.

IC railroaders in Birmingham were not eager for new locomotives, and my arrival there was not too warmly greeted. It seems that the Birmingham District was its own little world, and steam had been bumped out of there by black GP9's, which in four-unit sets handled the hilly, curving terrain pretty well. The only experience they'd had with "orange engines" had been a handful of the 3040-series GP40's that had been brought in when Chicago got the brilliant idea of replacing four 1750-h.p. GP9's with two 3000-h.p. GP40's. While that may work in theory on the flat main line, the Birmingham District is

a tractive-effort rather than a horsepower railroad, where you simply need lots of wheels on the rails to pull the hills. The powerful but slippery GP40's were complete failures on the Birmingham District, and when the local folks heard that we were going to "take away their black Geeps" and give them more of "those damned orange engines," they weren't too happy.

The SD40A's began arriving, and I had to shuttle back and forth between Haleyville and Birmingham to ride them. Since train schedules weren't convenient for return rides in either direction, I often rode a bus to or from Haleyville or Jasper. Although the Frisco had managed to dump its last Kansas City-Birmingham train, the *Southland*, in 1967, the line still had IC passenger service in the form of the every-other-day *City of Miami* between Chicago and Florida, southbound into Birmingham at 10:20 p.m. and northbound at 3:40 in the morning. Prior to its being cut back to a Chicago-Carbondale service on June 3, 1969, the *Seminole* had been a daily train between Chicago and Jacksonville, Florida, hitting Birmingham at 7:50 a.m. southbound and 7 p.m. northbound. Because the *City of Miami* schedule closely matched that of freight SE-1, I never got a passenger cab ride over the Birmingham District.

EAST THOMAS YARD in Birmingham, Alabama, was a joint facility of IC and Frisco and the domain of black Geeps equipped with "Birmingham Train Control" for negotiating the trackage rights over Frisco and Southern. In late August 1969, U30B 5003 (below) **had slipped into East Thomas as a trailing unit.**

SOUTHBOUND SE-1 paused for the crew change at Haleyville on August 31, 1969, with three new SD40A's. However, lead unit 6015, making its first trip, was not loading, and the approaching rain would put the 6009 and 6007 to the test 65 miles south on Adamsville Mountain.

A Night on Adamsville Mountain

The new SD40A's were being applied in three-unit sets on SE-1 and BC-4 and working pretty well, but the engineers were still skeptical of them. The big units finally proved themselves to the Birmingham District on the rainy Sunday night of August 31, 1969. Hotshot SE-1 had rolled into Haleyville just before dark, about three hours late behind the 6015, 6009 and 6007 with 74 loads and 30 empties at 7,406 tons. That would have been a very heavy train for the traditional four Geeps and was a substantial load for even three SD40A's.

But SE-1 was having its problems. The 6015 was making its first trip and was not "loading." That is, the diesel engine was running fine, but it was not delivering any electrical power to the motors. It was the only unit in the set, however, to have the Birmingham Train Control package functioning and needed to be kept in the lead (while all the SD40A's were equipped with the special train control equipment, not all of them had it properly set up yet and calibrated for service). Since the 6015 was not loading, the engineer had no ammeter to use to judge his throttle handling.

The two trailing units howled as SE-1 strained out of Haleyville into the windy and rainy night. In the warm and comfortable cab I unfolded the "bed sheet" SD40A wiring diagram and began to do what little I could to locate the source of the trouble (the problem was later found to be a faulty relay contact in the load regulator circuit). With 7,406 tons and only 6000 horsepower, we were in for a slow trip. Flatland railroads generally regard one horsepower per ton to be adequate power for a 50-m.p.h. road freight, while a fast railroad like the Cotton Belt would assign 4.75 horsepower per ton to a *Blue Streak Merchandise*. With only two units pulling, 7,406 tons trailing and 200 tons of useless SD40A on the point, SE-1 was definitely no *Streak*.

The Southern and Frisco segments of the Birmingham District were rugged pieces of railroad, with lots of curves and a sawtooth profile that included numerous short grades in excess of 1 percent. The ruling grade, however, was Adamsville Mountain, just north of Birmingham with a six-mile southbound grade that hit 1.3 percent—N&W's notorious Blue Ridge Grade in Virginia was nine miles of only 1.2 percent! The Adamsville grade begins at Lindbergh, Milepost 717.3, with a one-mile pull of 1.1 percent, flattens out briefly at Milepost 718.1 and then picks back up at Milepost 718.7 with a 1.3 percent haul to the top at Milepost 723.2 in Adamsville.

Right in the middle of that six-mile hill is "*Sunchaser* Curve" where an IC 4-8-2 and the every-third-day Miami-Chicago passenger train No. 8, the *Sunchaser*, derailed just after

midnight on April 25, 1948. The baffles in the locomotive's tender had broken loose, and the water sloshing around as the engine came down through the many curves finally got just the right harmonics set up on the curve at Milepost 720 to flip the tender off the track, taking the locomotive and train with it, resulting in two deaths (the engineer and a female passenger) and 31 injuries. Adamsville Mountain was no joke.

As we encountered the 1.1 percent grade our speed began to sag. The engineer needed to know how many amps the motors were pulling, so he sent me back to the trailing units to see if either had a working radio; luckily, the second unit did. I sat in the engineer's seat on the 6009 and began to give him amp readings on the radio—this wasn't as easy as it sounds, since these particular ammeters had no numbers on them but used a color-coded quadrant to depict the short-time ratings. (As the speed of a diesel-electric locomotive drops, the amps pulled by the motors increases, and since amps equate to heat, you can only draw high amperage for a limited time before you risk overheating and damaging the motors. The ammeter usually includes a "short-time rating" chart that shows how long you can work at any given amp load without causing damage.)

I was pretty sure that "the peg" on the ammeter was 1400 amps, and before long we were down to 9 m.p.h. pulling what I'd esti-

mate to be roughly 1350 amps—just shy of the peg. Now, darned few locomotives can pull that kind of amperage on dry rail without slipping (a GP40 gets real skittery around 1000 amps, for example), but at 417,000 pounds—the SD40A's being the heaviest locomotives ever owned by IC—the six motors kept the horsepower per motor down to 500, and the IDAC (Instantaneous Detection And Correction) wheel-slip system was very effective. On the wet rail, the units were down on their hands and knees, but with the lead unit laying down dry sand and the IDAC working perfectly, the 6009 hung onto that high amperage like the needle was painted on the dial—on a lesser locomotive, the amp needle would have been jumping all over the place as the wheels would slip, grab and lurch, over and over again.

The turbos were still howling in Run-8 as we were deep into the shortest short time rating. With about a minute left before we'd have to shut down, I asked the engineer on the radio how far we had to go.

"The crest is at that crossbuck about 200 yards ahead," he replied. We were about a hundred yards away when time ran out. "Shall I shut 'em down?" he asked.

The book says yes, but I felt that if those engines "fell down" on Adamsville Mountain, we'd never hear the end of it, and they'd have a bad reputation from then on. I asked the engineer, "How long before we're over the top?"

THE SD40A's proved to be excellent motive power for the Birmingham District. In August 1974, the shine was off the 6019 (the first unit of the second order of SD40A's, 6019-6023, delivered in January 1970) as it idled at Jackson, Tennessee, in the company of U33C 5053.

NORTHBOUND TRAIN 10, the *Shawnee* (the Carbondale-Chicago remnant of the *Seminole*), had an E8 in the lead on September 19, 1969, as it slowly approached Rantoul (above) while No. 1, the southbound *City of New Orleans*, made its station stop. A little farther up the line, the speedometer (left) was hovering at 86 m.p.h.—those E-units rode beautifully at high speed. A southbound freight led by SD40 6000 (below) met No. 10 at Kankakee. One of the benefits of working as an EMD field instructor was having a cab pass which permitted return rides on freight or passenger trains, and this particular trip was the result of having worked freight SE-1 between Chicago and Champaign the previous day.

"About a minute."

"Go for it, and as soon as you can, throttle back and get rid of those amps."

I stuck my head out the window and sniffed the air for the smell of hot motors, but all I got was a headful of rain. The SD40A's crawled over the top, and the amps dropped down as the speed picked up and the engineer notched back. Before long we were in full dynamics descending the south slope of Adamsville Hill.

I had one impressed crew on my hands. "I've never seen an engine that could dig in like that!" the fireman exclaimed after watching the performance on the ammeter in the third unit. The engineer was equally enthusiastic, "These are the best engines I've ever run!"

When we showed up at Thomas Junction, we were greeted by a red signal and a disbelieving yardmaster. "What're you doing here?" he demanded on the radio.

"We pulled Adamsville Mountain and just kept comin'," the engineer smugly replied.

"Well, hell, when we heard you had only two working units, we figured you'd be out there all night; I don't even have a track open for you yet."

Score: SD40A's 1 / Yardmaster 0. Nobody in Birmingham ever whined about losing their black Geeps again.

Back to Markham

On Tuesday, September 2, I got instructions to return to Chicago, and I spent the next few weeks keeping tabs on the SD40A's running to Birmingham and the 3060-series GP40's working west to Omaha. It gave me the opportunity to get in some cab riding on the main line. On September 17, the 6018—the last of the SD40A's—was delivered from LaGrange, and the next day I rode it south to Champaign on SE-1 with my old friends 6015 and 6007. Since there was no return ride handy, I stayed over in Champaign and rode back to Chicago the next morning on No. 10, the *Shawnee*—the remnant of the *Seminole*. Returning from another freight trip to Champaign, I caught E6 4001 in the lead on No. 8, now called the *Illini*, and got in some real 90-m.p.h. running aboard one of my all-time favorite locomotives.

I also made a couple of trips west to Freeport on CC-1, including one on October 9 with GP40 prototype 433A leading the 3065, 3066 and 3060. I got quite a kick out of photographing my former apartment in Rockford

IOWA DIVISION manifest CC-1 was ready to depart Markham Yard (right) shortly after dawn on October 9, 1969, with EMD's prototype GP40 433A leading three new IC 3060-series GP40's. The author rode this train west to Freeport, Illinois.

THE FREEPORT depot (left) was framed in the window of GP40 433A on CC-1. The SW1 had brought the C&NW local over from Rockford and was parked where, some two decades earlier, North Western's Chicago-Freeport passenger local used to tie up with its unusual Baldwin-built combination locomotive/baggage car unit.

through the cab window of the 433A (page 34). From Wallace Yard in Freeport, I got a return trip on Second CC-6 with the 3061, 3001 and 3042.

Motive-Power Games

IC had purchased the ten 3060-series GP40's for use in a Chicago-North Platte motive-power pool with Union Pacific that had been inaugurated in February 1969. The units, as I've mentioned before, were deluxe versions with dynamic brakes and UP-compliant appliances. The only problem with the pool was that IC had some bridges on the Iowa Division west of Fort Dodge over which it had restricted six-motor units—like the UP's "Standard Locomotive," the SD40. This meant that the UP would have to reciprocate

with four-motor power in its share of the pool. And the UP didn't *have* any new four-motor power.

My Weekly Activity Report for October 4, 1969, contained a note at the end, reflecting on the fact that since the middle of September my work at Markham Roundhouse had dealt exclusively with SD40A's. I quote:

"The IC has been running the SD40A's almost exclusively on BC-4 and SE-1 in and out of Markham. The variations in the units indicate that they are being used somewhere else south of here, but they almost always arrive in a three-unit set on BC-4 and are turned immediately and sent out an hour later on SE-1. If the '6007, 6008 & 6018 in and out on BC-4 and SE-1' in my report seems a bit brief, it's only because that is about all I see of them.

A POWER POOL with Union Pacific between Chicago and North Platte was inaugurated in February 1969 and resulted in the purchase of the ten 3060-series GP40's with dynamic brakes and UP appliances. In March 1969, before the new GP40's were delivered, CC-1 was westbound at 21st Street with IC GP40 3019 leading a set of UP cab and booster GP30's.

"You may ask, 'What about those ten GP40's of Order 7171?' I was beginning to wonder about that myself. A check of the units in and out of Markham indicated that the last new GP40 left Markham on September 19 on CC-1 westbound. Ever since then, the entire fleet of new GP40's, 3060-3069, has been on the Union Pacific and has never returned to IC rails!

"P.S. In return for the brand new GP40's, the IC has been getting UP GP20's, GP30's, GP35's, high-nose U25B's and even one very weary—dead—Alco DL640.

"Somebody's being had!"

The UP had glommed onto those GP40's, and a photo later showed up in the June 1970 *Trains* Magazine of five of them—half the fleet in one set—pulling Cajon Pass out of Los Angeles with the LAX (and recent observations confirm that Cajon is slightly west of North Platte, Nebraska). With the collection of four-motor junk that Omaha was sending the IC in return, Uncle Pete was definitely getting the better end of the deal. Mr. Harriman would have been proud. (Of course, this was all being accounted for on a unit- or horsepower-per-day basis, and IC *was* using the UP units all the way to New Orleans upon occasion—but there's little doubt that UP was getting better service out of brand new GP40's than the IC was out of even the best of the UP GP30's.)

The status of the UP motive-power pool

had gotten so silly that my morning routine at the Markham invariably included a round of, "Okay, Boyd, what's this?"

Knowing I was a railfan familiar with non-EMD products, the IC foreman would march me out to the roundhouse and point at some piece of Armour yellow alien hardware and ask that question. The high-nose GE U25B and Alco DL640 were particularly fun to explain. This was real culture shock for a man who until a year or so ago had spent his entire motive-power career with black Geeps.

Of course, the ultimate practical joke the UP had played on the IC was in June 1969, a few months before I was assigned there. Taking literally the ban on six-motor units west of Fort Dodge, somebody noted that no mention had been made to forbid *eight*-motor units and slipped DD35A No.77 into Chicago on CC-8. The horrified IC spent about three weeks trying to figure out how to get that monster back to the UP without running it west of Fort Dodge. In the meantime, it was spotted making a number of trips between Chicago and St. Louis, and I later heard that it went back to the UP via St. Louis.

We finally got our GP40's back and completed the After Service Inspections on them and the SD40A's in early October 1969. Shortly thereafter I left the motive-power madness of Markham and was reassigned to Pine Bluff, Arkansas, and the relative sanity of more SP SD45's on the Cotton Belt. ✦

THE UNION PACIFIC power pool brought a bizarre collection of four-motor power into the Markham roundhouse, precipitating considerable culture shock in a mechanical staff that had dealt with little other than EMD power since the end of steam. Weight limits on a bridge west of Fort Dodge restricted the pool to four-motor units, which obliged UP to supply only older power, since all of its "new" power was six-motor (mostly SD40's) or larger. One of the more unusual visitors to Markham was high-nosed GE U25B 631 (left) in September 1969, while the most-common UP pool units were UP GP30's, such as shown on the previous page. Another unusual visitor was UP Alco DL640 676, shown in the roundhouse (below) spotted between a black Geep and Paducah's first rebuild, switcher 200. Because of the motive-power in-equities—new IC GP40's versus UP "junk"—the power pool lasted only a year.

CHAPTER 5

A Grande Time

A few months before I was assigned there by EMD, the IC had entered a time of motive-power chaos that will be remembered as probably the most colorful period in its post-steam history. Not only was the arch-conservative black Geep Main Line of Mid-America being subjected to chop-noses, turbochargers, Alcos, GE's, orange paint and UP run-throughs, but it was also dealing with that most alien of locomotive concepts: the F-unit! While no stranger to the "covered wagon" carbodies of its E-units, the IC actually rostered three Alco RS2's before it ever saw its first covered-wagon freight unit.

During the late 1960's the IC was finally beginning to come to grips with the realities of modern railroading and realizing that it would take more than a pair of GP9's to competitively handle meat trains off the UP, Wisconsin Electric unit coal trains and new *Fastback* intermodals. And the older Geeps that were being put through the Paducah Shop rebuild program were unavailable for service during their often lengthy reconstruction, further tightening the motive-power situation. New units like the big Alcos and GE's and GP40's and SD40A's were a substantial help, but even more power was needed.

Thus the IC turned to the locomotive leasing market. Since the early 1960's, the Denver & Rio Grande Western had been replacing its massive fleet of F7's with GP30's, GP35's, GP40's and now SD45's, and by early 1969 it was putting many of those F7's up for lease or sale. In May 1969, the IC jumped in for a lease of ten F7 B-units (5702, 5703, 5712, 5713, 5722, 5723, 5742, 5743, 5752 and 5753) and

followed up in July with eight F7 cab units (5704, 5714, 5724, 5731, 5734, 5741, 5744 and 5754). These colorful Colorado covered wagons were apparently in very good condition and soon found their way onto freight assignments out of Markham Yard and were particularly common on trains to St. Louis.

By the summer of 1969 when I was working out of Markham for EMD, the Rio Grande units were very much in evidence, sometimes running in matched sets—A-B-B-A, of course—or mixed with the UP power pool units. When work and weather permitted, I took the opportunity to chase and photograph the Rio Grandes, and on one memorable occasion, September 5, 1969, Rio Grande F7 5731 headed south out of Markham trailing two UP GP30's and a GP35 (page 91).

Also in May of 1969 the IC had briefly leased a handful of F-units from Precision Engineering Corporation of Mount Vernon, Illinois, including a couple of ex-SP F7's and ex-Great Northern F3 367A in Big Sky Blue. But this was just the beginning.

In October 1969, the first of ten Bessemer & Lake Erie F7 cab and booster units showed up. The handsome orange-and-black ore-haulers included F7 cabs 712-714, 716 and 717 and boosters 713B, 714B, 717B, 718B and 725B.

Two months later, Precision Engineering leased to IC eleven former-Katy F-units including four F3A's (64A, 64C, 67A and 68C), an F3B (68B), four F7A's (70C, 74C, 75A and 77C) and two FP7A's (78A and 79C). Along with the Rio Grandes and B&LE's, these units all called Markham home and worked throughout northern Illinois. They even ful-

---

LEASED DENVER & RIO GRANDE WESTERN F7A 5734 was a strange bedfellow to somber-black IC units at Markham Yard in September 1969, but it and other leased "covered wagons" presented a "Grande" opportunity for railfans.

RIO GRANDE F7's added an unexpected dash of color to the IC motive-power scene in the summer of 1969. The 5724 (right) **had an A-B-B-A set idling the night away beneath the new water tower at the Markham engine terminal in September, while in early August an A-B set** (below) **had been roaring up Alworth Hill west of Rockford with CFS-3.**

filled my lifelong dream of seeing F-units on the Gruber through Dixon.

And just to let you know how highly the Illinois Central regarded the most powerful new locomotives on its roster, in January 1970, while still leasing more than two dozen F-units, the IC leased its six Alco C636's out to the Canadian Pacific!

Sanity Returns

IC's motive-power madness began to resolve itself in early 1970 when two things occurred: Deliveries commenced on 30 new locomotives, and the UP motive-power pool was cancelled on February 28. The new locomotives were five more SD40A's (6019-6023), five more deluxe GP40's (3070-3074) and 20

A PERFECT A-B-B-A SET of Rio Grande F7's had a St. Louis-bound freight on the Markham southbound departure tracks in September 1969. D&RGW F7 5731 was heading up another St. Louis train at Monee, Illinois, on September 5 (below) trailing two UP GP30's and a GP35—an incredible image for the Main Line of Mid-America!

COVERED WAGONS met at Homewood Tower in September 1969 as Rio Grande 5734 on an outbound St. Louis freight encountered a pair of IC E8's on No. 10, the *Shawnee*, at the south end of Markham Yard. In addition to the Rio Grandes, IC leased a number of units from Precision Engineering, including the Big Sky Blue GN F3 367-A and a gray SP F7B, shown at Markham (left) in July 1969. In October 1969, IC leased a batch of F-units from the Bessemer & Lake Erie; the 712 and a B-unit and a Katy F7A (below) were at Wallace Yard in Freeport, Illinois, in late July 1971.

GP38's (9500-9519). While the SD40A's joined their kin in the Birmingham pool, the GP40's went into general service, and the GP38's were assigned to the Iowa Division and became regulars on the Gruber.

Most of the B&LE units were gone by the end of 1969, and the last of the Rio Grande F-units was fixed up and sent to the Burlington Northern in May 1970, but some of the PECO/Katys hung on for about another year.

The IC's F-unit era was Grande while it lasted.

Don't Forget the Demonstrators

Being a dedicated EMD customer and located not far from the factory at LaGrange, IC had worked closely with EMD over the years in locomotive testing and development. Throughout the late 1960's, the IC had been the unofficial home for many of EMD's engineering test units. The prototype GP40 (the black 433A with flared radiator housings) had become a common sight mixed in with the new dynamic-brake-equipped GP40's. Also making frequent appearances on the IC was the first SD45, EMD's blue-and-white 4351, frequently accompanied by an engineering test car and blue-and-white F7 462 and a companion B-unit. In June 1970, EMD's newest and biggest showed up and quickly made Markham home: the 4200-h.p., 20-cylinder SD45X (SD55) 5740.

During that summer, the 5740 became a common sight on the servicing tracks along IC's huge new Woodcrest Shop, opened on May 18, 1970, which was replacing the old Markham Roundhouse, Burnham Shop and the 27th Street passenger roundhouse uptown. The immense $14 million Woodcrest

THE LAST PLACE the author ever expected to see F-units was on the Illinois Central through his hometown of Dixon, Illinois. In March 1970, Katy FP7 79C—a passenger unit, no less—was leading a mix of PECO/Katys and Bessemer F's north on No. 372 across the Seventh Street crossing (above) as the Dixon switch job's Geep idled on the Engine Track. On another day that month, 372 (below) had a Bessemer and three Katys rolling over the Rock River trestle. The Rio Grande F-units also showed up on the Gruber both in pure sets and mixed with Bessemers and Katys.—TWO PHOTOS, MIKE MCBRIDE

Shop (named after the adjoining communities of Homewood and Hazelcrest) put nearly a city block under roof and even included an indoor transfer table. North of the main shop was a running-service building, which had two indoor tracks for fueling and washing incoming locomotives. Once the new shop complex was up and working, the old Markham Roundhouse was bulldozed into oblivion.

From black Geeps in the steam-era roundhouse to shiny orange SD40A's and an EMD SD45X at the new running service building, the shift from Markham Roundhouse to Woodcrest Shop was more than just a change in name. It was the symbol of the Illinois Central's last hours of glory. ◈

WALLACE ENGINE terminal (above) **had leased B&LE F7's between a new GP38 and a veteran SW7 in July 1970. The 20 new GP38's were delivered in February 1970 with dynamic brakes and the "L-shaped" windshield; four 9500's had CC-6 accelerating out of Freeport** (below) **in July 1970. On a hazy day three months later** (right) **two Katy F3's were northbound at the Squires Avenue crossing near the Boyd home in Dixon.**

Demo Doin's

ELECTRO-MOTIVE DIVISION of General Motors had a good working relationship with IC and used the railroad for testing many of its new units. The black GP40 prototype 433A saw extensive service on the IC; it was on a test set at the 27th Street Roundhouse in Chicago (top) in 1965. EMD's SD45 demonstrators 4353 and 4354 (above) were at Wallace Yard in February 1967 after coming up the Gruber from Clinton; IC later bought prototype SD45 4351. The 4200-h.p. prototype SD45X 5740 (right) was on a test set at the Woodcrest Shop in 1970.

CHAPTER 6

On May 15, 1970, my career with the Electro-Motive Division of General Motors came to a sudden end. The Service Department was undergoing restructuring, and I'd already been transferred from LaGrange to the Northeastern Region, headquartered in New York City. I was called to New York from my assignment on the Penn Central at Gibson, Indiana, and informed that my job was being eliminated as part of an overall cutback. In reality, I suspect that my railfanning and magazine-article writing had not been looked upon with favor by some folks in the Northeastern Region office, and although I'd been doing a good job as a field instructor, my lack of college credentials would limit further advancement.

I was not particularly distressed. I figured that I'd conned General Motors out of nearly three years of the best fun a railfan could have and had gotten paid for it.

Over the next couple of weeks I contacted most of the railroads in the Chicago area to find out if they had any openings for someone with my locomotive experience but came up blank. About that time Chet French (my longtime friend from Dixon who was now a conductor on the IC) told me that Trainmaster Pete Clayton was hiring brakemen at Freeport, Illinois. I couldn't pass up a chance to go "railroadin' for real" and made a bee-line for Freeport. Apparently Chet had put in a good word for me with Mr. Clayton, and I left Freeport with a job application and an appointment for a company physical.

Here again Chet was a big help. He advised me to get the physical and mark up for my student trips as rapidly as possible, because five others were being hired at the same time. My permanent seniority in the group would be determined by how quickly I got the student trips completed and was certified ready for work. Then he took me over to the yard in Dixon and gave me a quick course in being a brakeman. He showed me how to line and lock a switch, set and release hand brakes, connect air hoses and cut in the air. He also explained how to bleed the train line for switching and showed me the basic hand signals for both day and night.

After passing the physical in Chicago, I headed immediately back to Freeport and marked up for my first student trip. I would be required to make one round trip into Chicago and a round trip down to Clinton and work one trick in Wallace Yard (Freeport). I made the trips as quickly as I legally could, getting the required eight hours rest between jobs. Chet's instructions were put to good use, and I got excellent marks from each conductor I worked with. I was officially marked up for work on July 28, 1970. Only one of the six students got on the board ahead of me.

Wallace Yard

Since new hires don't always live in Freeport, the railroad had a list of private individuals who would rent sleeping rooms to railroaders. I got a nice room in the home of the grandmotherly Daisy Kirchner (on Pleasant Street, no less), not far from Wallace Yard. She had three upstairs rooms she rented to railroaders. We didn't take any meals there, but the phone ringing and our traipsing in and out at all hours didn't seem to bother her.

Wallace Yard was my home terminal, and

THE "FIRST MEAT TRAIN," WC-2 out of Iowa, had overtaken an eastbound Chain Gang Extra at Hawthorne (nine miles west of Chicago) on August 15, 1971, and was framed in the back door of the Extra's caboose in the hazy morning light.

THE AUTHOR had his "block" placed on the Wallace extra board (right) on July 28, 1970, after making three student trips, including one to Clinton, during which he crossed the Rock River (below) at Dixon aboard black Geeps. In August and in front of his Freeport rooming house (above), he was ready for work.—MIKE SCHAFER

my seniority was both as a brakeman (working road jobs) and as a switchman (working in the yard). My freight territory included the main line 140 miles east to Markham Yard in Chicago, the Gruber 164 miles south to Clinton and the 60-mile branch north to Madison, Wisconsin. I could also be called for yard jobs at Wallace, Rockford and my old hometown of Dixon. My territory for passenger service extended west to Dubuque, Iowa, though I didn't figure there was much likelihood of exercising that—after a decade on the railroad, even

Chet had never worked a passenger job. Being one of the youngest brakemen from the standpoint of seniority, I went immediately to the extra board.

Wallace Yard is located on the north side of the Iowa Division main line about two miles west of downtown Freeport. In the early 1960's, the huge steam-era roundhouse east of the downtown passenger station had been closed, and the 100-foot turntable was mounted on freight-car trucks and rolled like a boxcar out to a new pit prepared for it on the south side of the main line at Wallace where the new diesel-servicing facility was located.

Wallace was actually two seven-track yards side by side with a couple of common connector tracks between them. The East Yard, adjacent to the main line, handled eastbound and Gruber trains, with its lead worked from the east end in front of the yard office. The West Yard, which handled westbound and Madison Branch trains, was on the north side of the yard office and was worked from a lead on the west end. A pair of EMD switchers was assigned to Wallace, and they handled the 7:59 a.m. and 3:59 and 11:59 p.m. yard jobs, plus an afternoon "Kelly Job," which worked Wallace, the downtown local yard and the Kelly-Springfield Tire plant east of town.

I got to know that midnight yard job pretty well. We'd begin by "bleeding The Bullet"—No. 73, the Chicago-Fort Dodge-Sioux Falls freight CFS-3—which usually got in sometime between 7 p.m. and midnight. This first task was to walk the length of the train, pulling the bleed levers to release the air from the brake reservoirs so that the cars could be flat-switched and "kicked" with no air brakes. Then we'd go out on the west lead and make up the westbound continuation of CFS-3 and, for the next morning, the Madison Branch train. Anything CFS-3 had brought in that was headed south or destined for local Freeport customers was "put to the Connection" to be worked in the East Yard. Then after a break we'd go to work in the East Yard, making up the "Long Gruber" (freight 373 to Clinton) and the "Short Gruber" (the Mendota Turn local). About dawn we'd stand by to handle any set-offs or pick-ups needed by eastbound No. 78, the "first meat train." If 78 wasn't going to show before 8 a.m., a good yardmaster would usually let the midnight switch crew go home as soon as their work was done, sometimes as early as 3 or 4 a.m.

One of the things you learn when you hire out on a railroad is that every track has a

name or number. In Wallace, in addition to the numbered yard tracks, were things like the Pocket, the Connection and the Run-Around. The five tracks in front of the yard office, for instance, were the Tank Lead (though the old locomotive water tank was long gone), the Caboose Track, the Switch Lead and the Westbound and Eastbound mains. As a railfan, learning the names was fascinating, because most of them had steam-era origins.

Learning to switch cars in a yard was pretty easy on the IC, because the switch lists used "Station Codes" that indicated the route and milepost. The main line west was the "W"

A CHICAGO-BOUND Extra was viewed from the Route 26 bridge (top left) easing out of Wallace Yard on the eastbound main in August 1970. Wallace is on the west side of Freeport. The "high switch" on the westbound main gives access to the East Yard lead in front of the yard office and to the West Yard lead behind it. A pair of Geeps on a Gruber job had the yard pretty well tied up (below) when it got tangled in the crossovers in front of the yard office. The piggyback train is on Track 2 of the East Yard. Framed in the fireman's window of a westbound high-nose Geep (left center), East Junction is where the Gruber to Clinton swung south and the double track through Freeport ended. A two-unit job was waiting on the Gruber while another train held on the eastbound main for the traffic to clear in March 1971.

BUCKBEE SIDING on the east side of Rockford could be a busy place. In September 1970, eastbound CC-6 (right) was framed in the fireman's window of the GP40 leading westbound CC-1 in the siding. The 3067 on CC-6 was working hard uphill past the Rockford Standard Furniture Company. The fireman's rear-view mirror reflected CC-1's train on the curve. The crossover in the foreground allowed the local switcher to make runaround movements when working the Rockford Belt Line industrial loop, whose east end is visible at left.

C&NW'S West Chicago-to-Freeport "Pumpkin Vine" line paralleled the IC at Buckbee, and in August 1970 (above) IC CC-6 was snarling uphill as it overtook a Geep ambling eastward with the C&NW local out of Rockford bound for Belvidere and West Chicago.

line, and all you had to do was line up the "W" numbers in order—W127 Lena, W145 Apple River, W153 Scales Mound, etc. Anything bound for W276 Waterloo or beyond was simply regarded as a "High West" and blocked as a through car to be classified at Waterloo. Eastbound, the "W's" would be blocked in descending order (W87 Rockford, W35 Munger, etc.) with anything east of W10 Hawthorne simply designated as a "0" for Markham Yard. The Madison Branch was the "R" line (Madison was R62), and the Gruber was the "A" line (Dixon was A35 and Clinton A162).

As for road jobs, we had a daily-except-Sunday day local to Madison, the daytime 373/372 to and from Clinton, and four Second Class "dispatch" freights plus Third Class local 91/92 each way between Freeport and Chicago.

Although the employee timetable had authorized schedules for four dispatch freights in each direction, there were usually only three trains, and the symbols could be shifted among the numbered schedules as needed (meat train CC-6 ran as No. 76 on most days, but it could show up on the earlier schedule as No. 78, for instance). The schedule slot that didn't have a train was usually annulled by train order or given to the local, whose Third Class schedule would then be annulled. Two or three days a week they'd call a "Chain Gang" Extra freight to fill the vacant slot or run as a first or second section of a scheduled train.

The meat trains to Chicago were covered by six "preferred crews" who were assigned to specific trains. There were two eastbound meat trains in the morning, WC-2 and CC-6, and CC-8 in the evening, usually running as Nos. 78, 76 and 74, respectively. Westbound there was CC-1 out of Markham around dawn, CFS-3 out in the afternoon and the hot CAC-5 in the evening, usually running as 71, 73 and 75.

Working off the extra board, we could be called for any vacancy that occurred on any yard or road job. There were usually five or six men on the board at any given time, and it could "turn over" in anything from eight hours to three days. The crew caller in the yard office could usually predict how fast things would move, but you always had to stay close to a telephone and not stray more than an hour away from Freeport.

This was the transition era between five-man and four-man crews, when the railroad was in the process of eliminating the fireman on road jobs. Certain jobs, mostly locals, still required a fireman, but on the road jobs they were optional, to be filled only if a protected man was available. A typical road crew would be made up of an engineer, a conductor, a flagman (rear brakeman), a head brakeman and maybe a fireman. The extra-board trainman usually worked as head brakeman and rode the locomotive instead of the caboose. I didn't mind that one bit!

"Drive 'Em, Benny"

On one of my first trips on CC-6 into Chicago, I encountered engineer Benny Beirau (pronounced BY-roo), a pleasant old-timer who wore steam-era coveralls and the traditional cap. Benny was a cautious fellow, who was very conscientious about safety and signals and speed restrictions (he'd usually take a 25 m.p.h. slow order at 20 or less just to be safe). But when the railroad was clear and the signals were green, Benny liked to let 'em roll, and some of the fastest trips I ever made down into Rockford were with Benny—capped off with the cheap thrill of grabbing train orders at 35 m.p.h. right beneath the overhanging eaves of the Rockford passenger station.

That first trip with Benny was rather uneventful, and the small talk was minimal until we were rolling downhill into Genoa. As a railfan I knew that there used to be a coal chute for the steam locomotives at the siding at Hart just west of town, and the ramp for the hopper track was still evident in the weeds. As we approached the site at about 65 m.p.h., I looked over at Benny, waved him a quick highball and shouted across the cab, "Highball the coal chute, Benny."

Without blinking an eye, he dutifully repeated, "Highball the coal chute." Then he paused a moment and gave me the strangest look. "How would a young fella' like you know about the coal chute?"

I confessed that I was a railfan and knew all about 2400's and 1100's and all sorts of steam stuff. Well, just like a couple of years earlier with Parky Parkman and Splinter Brannan on the Tallahatchie District, I made an instant friend.

Given his peculiar reputation for both caution and speed, Benny was greeted over the radio by everybody on the railroad with the same salute, "Drive 'em, Benny!" And he'd always calmly reply, "Drive 'em."

Sometimes Benny's cautious side would drive you nuts. On every trip to Markham he'd warn me to be on the lookout for one particular signal near Kensington that liked to hide behind some wires. His warning was always the same. As we entered C Yard at Harvey on the north end of Markham on one memorable trip, he radioed his regular flagman, John Woodward, "Now, Johnny, you be sure to tell me when the caboose is in the clear."

Woodward replied with just a touch of sarcasm, "Yeah, Benny, just like every trip since 1964, I'll tell you when the hind end is in the clear."

Benny proceeded into Track 7, reassured.

Westward Ho, the wagons!

It was about my second month on the railroad when I found myself working CC-6 into Chicago with engineer Russ Melnick, who I hadn't seen around Freeport before. Russ said that he'd been working the Broadview Job out of Hawthorne for the last few years and had just moved back to Freeport. This was his first road trip since then, and we had no fireman.

I didn't give the matter much thought until we came across the Rock Island at Clark Street and headed east toward Chicago's lakefront on the St. Charles Air Line. When we reached the ramp where the line turns south to Markham Yard, Russ gave me a puzzled look and brought the train to a halt.

"What's this?" he asked.

"It's the connection with the main line to Markham," I replied.

"Markham . . . I've never been there!" Russ exclaimed. "The last time I worked east we turned left here and tied up at Congress Street." (The new wye had been opened in June 1968, and following that, the Iowa trains ran 18 miles south down the main line into Markham rather than a mile north into Congress Street).

About this time, the conductor, whose caboose was hanging out over Rock Island's busy commuter line at Clark Street, came on the

radio asking why we had stopped.

"I've never been to Markham," Russ explained, "and I don't have a fireman."

Knowing that I was a recent hire, the conductor asked, "Boyd, how many trips have you made down there?"

"Five or six."

"Think you can handle it? All you have to do is read the signals and watch for the Harvey switchtender at Markham. If you don't think you can do it, I'll come on up to the engines."

"I'll give it a shot. If we encounter anything we don't understand, we'll get on the radio or stop," I replied. "Let's go for it."

"Okay, just be careful."

I was beginning to be thankful for Benny Beirau's careful instructions. There is one place just below Kensington where the eight or so tracks do a little jog to the right, and it displaces the visual alignment by one track. A real test of nerves is to be making 50 m.p.h. south at night on Track 4 while staring directly into the headlight of a 75-m.p.h. northbound passenger train on Track 3—that tiny green signal doesn't carry much authority compared to a Mars light in your face!

We made our way down that multi-track thoroughfare to the hand-thrown switches at Harvey at the north end of Markham's C Yard and got the switchtender's highball onto the receiving yard lead. "Put yourself in Track 9," the yardmaster instructed us.

The only problem is that there are no numbers on the switch stands, and there are a couple of named tracks that look like ladder tracks before the numbered tracks begin. But I knew the secret to C Yard. Benny had told me: There's a line of light poles down the middle of the yard that look like giant "11's", and they're just beyond Track 11. Find the poles and count toward you . . . Track 11, Track 10, Track 9. We put that train away like a couple of old-timers.

The next day was even more interesting. After laying over in the motel in Homewood, we reported to the Markham diesel house to pick up our power to take home on CFS-3. There on the ready track was a three-unit set of red PECO/Katy F-units. F3A 64C led, trailed elephant-style by F7A 75A and an F7B.

This was going to be a fun trip. I had my camera in my grip and walked across a couple of tracks to frame up a portrait shot in the perfect sunlight. I just got the camera up for the first shot when a Jeep screeched up beside me, and I had one irate IC railroad cop all over me. "You're trespassing here, and photography is forbidden!" he screamed. "Get out of here right now before I put you under arrest," he demanded and pointed toward the parking lot.

"Relax, I'm an employee," I calmly replied.

"I don't care if you're Wayne A. Johnston! Get the hell outta' here."

I put my camera away and headed toward the locomotives. That almost pushed the guy over the edge. "Where do you think you're going?" he sputtered.

"Over to 73's power; I'm working that job out of here." He couldn't quite handle that.

"Well then, still get the hell outta' here—and make it snappy!"

Getting it "outta' here" wasn't quite as simple as it looked. The two cab units were facing south with the blind B-unit on the north end, and we had to go north. But the 64C had no radio, and between us Russ and I had only my hand set. He could pick up a pack set radio at the yard office, but that was at the other end of Markham Yard.

I couldn't "ride the point" on the back of the B-unit, because on the first curve I'd be out of Russ' sight. I would have to stay in the cab

KATY F3 64C and two other PECO-leased Katy F-units were on CFS-3 out of Markham Yard in early September 1970, and the Chicago skyline made a fine sight (left) framed in the covered wagon's windshield as the train approached the "temporary" bridge built in the early 1920's over the electrified commuter line at 23rd Street. At GM&O's "Drawbridge" interlocking at Bridgeport (below) CFS-3 stopped to let the outbound *Abraham Lincoln* head west behind a rather shabby E7.

and play fireman, watching down the left side and trying to see around three covered wagons. We began easing backwards, and the first curve was in my direction. Then suddenly the B-unit, which was still out of Russ' view, began to turn away from me. "Hold it!" I shouted.

I scrambled back to see where we were going and found our B-unit with its open coupler knuckle interlocked with—but not touching—the front coupler of an E9. I got out to where Russ could see me, gave him a "go ahead" and realigned the switch. Then I walked down the lead around the next couple of curves to make sure all switches were lined for us and went back to the cab. We gingerly backed up to the mid-yard wye with no more problems, turned the units and headed for our train in C Yard.

Before long we were bound for Freeport. I got quite a kick out of seeing the familiar Chicago skyline framed in the curved windows of an F3. We got nailed by the Rock Island at Clark Street and again at the drawbridge over the South Fork spur of the Chicago River at Bridgeport interlocking, where we were overtaken by an E7 on GM&O's *Abraham Lincoln*.

Finally out of the terminal district and rambling up the hill toward Plato Center, Russ asked if I'd ever run a freight train. I told him that I had on a couple of occasions, and he offered to let me try my hand at it. Thus I wound up the trip by throttling the F-units all the way to Rockford.

As they say in the beer commercials, "It doesn't get any better than this."

Baggage Man on the Hawkeye

I'd only been on the railroad about two weeks when I walked into the caller's office at Wallace one day to see how I stood. "You're second out, and you'll probably get the midnight switch engine," caller Mike Hanna told me.

Puzzled, I asked, "What's getting called before me?"

"The baggage man on the passenger train is starting his vacation today, and I've got to call a deadhead in 20 minutes to cover the job for one trip. That extra man ahead of you will get it, and you'll be up for that hole on the midnight job."

Not really knowing what I was asking, but managing accidentally to phrase it in just the right words, I inquired, "Is that an open job?"

AUTHOR BOYD managed to catch one round trip as baggage man on the *Hawkeye*, between Dubuque, Iowa, and Chicago in August 1970. At 2:25 a.m. he posed for this photo just before No. 12 departed Dubuque. —MIKE SCHAFER

"It is, but you'd never hold it," he replied.

"But if I held it until the deadhead call, I'd have it for at least one trip, wouldn't I?"

"Well, yes. Nobody could bump you for tonight's job after the deadhead call time," he explained cautiously.

"Do you need a passenger uniform?"

"Nope, it's the baggage job, and all they require is neat and clean work clothes."

All I had to lose was another midnight yard job. "Mark me up!" I said, bidding on a job for the very first time in my railroad career.

"Anybody who walks in can bump you," he warned.

"I'll chance it." I waited around the nearly vacant yard office for the longest 20 minutes of my life—and not a soul came into the caller's office. At the prescribed time for the deadhead call, Mike announced, "Well, Jim, you've got the job. You won't hold it for more than one trip, but you've got it tonight." (I subsequently learned that I was bumped 25 minutes later by one very irate veteran who had forgotten about the deadhead call and thought the job would be his.)

Rather than take the deadhead to Dubuque on the westbound *Hawkeye* at 9:35 p.m. and have to sit for over three hours at Dubuque, I called up Mike Schafer in Rockford and asked if he'd like to ride the *Hawkeye* back from Iowa with me that night. He drove over to Freeport, and together we drove west to Dubuque in plenty of time for the 2:40 a.m. departure.

Number 12, the eastbound *Hawkeye*, rolled into Dubuque at 2:20 a.m., right on time, with high-speed Geep 9203, a gutted RPO car and two coaches. The inbound baggage man gave me a quick run-down of the work I'd need to do (handle a few pieces of checked baggage

and distribute the company mail) and took off with the rest of his crew for the hotel.

My job east of Dubuque worked a different pattern than the rest of the crew, who'd come out of Chicago earlier on No. 11 and were working 12 back to Freeport, where a new crew would come on, while I would work a round trip between Dubuque and Chicago. Conductor Bob Calkins was busy with passengers just before departure and paid little notice as Mike photographed me in the door of the mail car.

As soon as we were on the road, I went into the coach to ask Calkins a question about sorting the company mail. When he discovered that he had a totally inexperienced man on the job, he hit the ceiling and gave me a royal chewing-out for marking up on a job for which I wasn't qualified—and particularly for not taking the westbound deadhead so I could learn the job from the working baggage man!

I hid out in the mail car to stay out of Calkins' way until we reached Freeport, where he went off duty. Replacing him was Gary Hanson, a young conductor who was a good friend of Chet's. Gary was considerably more forgiving of my transgression, and once we were on the road again, his trainman, a pleasant veteran named Joe Dame, came up to check my work.

The small amount of baggage was clearly tagged and no problem, but the company mail was a bit more involved. There was a rack of mail-sorting slots on one inside wall that was marked for each station stop, and any mail that had to be set off was stashed in the proper slot. There were two destinations in Chicago that had big mail sacks: one each for Central Station and the office at Randolph Street. The mail that I picked up at each station was clearly marked, so sorting was no problem. By the time we got to Central Station, I was handling it like a pro. Following our 7:15 a.m. arrival in Chicago, we layed over in a hotel to get our rest for our trip west on No. 11 at 7 p.m.

Our little train with the 9203 had been turned and was waiting for us in Central Station that evening. A station baggage man was loading my car from a baggage wagon on the platform. I found the two big mail sacks marked for Waterloo and Fort Dodge, and I dutifully hung them on the wall hooks where I'd found them early that morning. There was only a small bundle of other company mail, which I quickly sorted out. Pretty soon I was enjoying the view out the open mail-car door as we zipped through the warm summer night, listening to the trusty 567 in the 9203.

I handed out and picked up a few pieces of

company mail at Broadview, Rockford and Freeport and even had a couple of pieces for the operator at Wallace Yard, where we made a brief stop. We were rocketing through the night west of Wallace when Joe Dame came up to the mail car asking if I'd gotten all the mail off for Wallace. "Of course," I replied.

"You sure?" he insisted. The operator says that the expense-account checks for the train-master are missing, and he was told that Randolph Street was sending them out tonight. Clayton's gonna' be furious."

"There were only a few pieces of mail put on," I explained, "and I've got those all sorted."

"Did you sort the big bags?"

"What do you mean, sort the big bags? Aren't they already sorted for Waterloo and Fort Dodge like the tags say?" I asked.

"Didn't you dump those bags out when you started?" he asked with a note of alarm.

"No, they were clearly tagged for Waterloo

and Fort Dodge. Why should I?"

"Because the Waterloo bag came from Central Station and the Fort Dodge bag from Randolph Street. That's where all the mail is; you have to dump those out and sort everything!"

You never saw such a pile of mail as the one I emptied onto that mail car floor 130 miles into the trip. There were Clayton's expense checks, and paperwork for Broadview, and stuff for Rockford and a couple of pieces for Warren, where we were just stopping. I could see the end of my railroading career postmarked "Dubuque."

Thank goodness for Joe Dame and Gary Hanson. Seeing my horror, Joe calmly pointed out that all I had to do was gather up every-

GARY HANSON (opposite) **was the conductor on the eastbound *Hawkeye* after the crew change at Freeport while the author was working as baggage man. Gary was one of the youngest conductors in Freeport District passenger service.**

DEPARTING CHICAGO on the gloomy August evening that the author was aboard as baggage man, the westbound *Hawkeye* descended the ramp (above) **from the St. Charles Air Line toward 21st Street and was photographed from the baggage car. Number 11 arrived at Dubuque** (left) **at 11:19 p.m. and made a 20-minute station stop before continuing west to Sioux City behind high-speed GP9 9203.**

The Best Crew

TWO MEMBERS of the crew on No. 12 when the author worked as baggage man in August 1970 were Trainman Joe Dame (left) **and Conductor Bob Calkins** (right). **When the author was having his troubles with the baggage job, Mr. Calkins was irate and Mr. Dame was very helpful. When Amtrak arrived on May 1, 1971, the** *Hawkeye* **was discontinued, and both Calkins and Dame returned to freight service. However, on February 14, 1974, when Amtrak and the State of Illinois reintroduced service to Dubuque as the** *Black Hawk,* **both returned to passenger duty. In 1975, a survey of Amtrak patrons conducted by** *Rail Travel News* **voted Conductor Bob Calkins and Assistant Conductor Joe Dame as the best crew on Amtrak. Although Bob Calkins had little patience with the inexperienced brakeman (the author) who bid the baggage job, his concern for his passengers was in the finest tradition of railroading.**

thing that we'd carried past its destination and take it off at Dubuque. Joe would be sure that the incoming baggage man (who wasn't deadheading but was driving to Dubuque like I had done) got the stuff distributed eastbound on No. 12. The crew'd be back into Chicago an hour before anybody came to work, and Clayton and the rest would never be aware that anything had happened. Joe advised, however, "Just stay away from Calkins for a while."

The incoming baggage man apparently kept his mouth shut, and I never heard a word about my disaster in the mail car. I was successful in staying clear of Bob Calkins for about a year until I caught him as conductor on the Madison job, but he didn't seem to remember me or that night on No. 12.

Chet and the Chain Gang

My phone rang at 4:10 p.m. on Friday, Sept. 18, 1970. Caller Bill Woods announced, "Boyd, you're called for a Chain Gang at 5:40 to turn at Harvey. I don't have a conductor yet."

That was good news. A Chain Gang was a freight Extra that would run to Markham and then return immediately to Freeport without laying over. It made for a long day, but got you two days' pay and a quick return to the extra board. When I got to the yard office at 5:30, there at the desk checking out the train orders and consist was my conductor—Chet French.

Chet had been working the Dixon Job since I'd hired out in July, and this was the first time I'd worked with him. Chet told the other (also new) brakeman, John Ellis, to work head end with engineer "Soup" Bons; I would work as flagman in the caboose with Chet.

He handed me the orders and consist; we were to run as Extra 9513 East with 97 cars for Markham. We had good power: new GP38 9513, black GP40 3008 and orange GP40 3069—all facing east, "elephant style". The train was waiting on the eastbound main, and Chet and I stayed in the yard office while Ellis and Soup got aboard and made the air test. The carman at the rear end radioed, "Okay, brakes are released on the Extra East."

Chet replied calmly, "Highball the 9513 East."

The three EMD's came to life, and we stepped outside to look the train over as it eased into motion. Everything looked good, and we easily snagged the caboose as it rolled by. From the rear platform I called on our radio, "Everybody on; highball the 9513 East."

There was a slight surge of slack, and the speed began to pick up. Our caboose was the 9916, a standard IC steel hack still in the red paint but fairly clean inside. Chet said, "It's

CHAIN GANG Extra 9513 East was on the eastbound main ready to depart Wallace Yard in Freeport on Friday, September 18, 1970. The "elephant-style" motive-power consist would not have time to be turned at Markham Yard in Chicago and would return to Wallace with the 3069 running long-hood-forward in the lead.

about time you learned the duties of a flagman; get the oil and fill the lamp." However, first I went onto the back platform and hung out the markers, which by now were, unfortunately, just reflectorized metal paddle boards. Then I got the oil can from the locker and filled the desk lamp. The new extended-vision cupola cabooses had electric lights, oil stoves and cushioned underframes, but the 9916 had an oil lamp, coal stove and solid draft gear.

After everything was squared away, we took our places in the cupola to keep an eye on the train. Chet and I had seen a lot of railroading since we'd met back in 1953 watching the 0-6-0 switch Bordens behind my granddad's house, but in all those years we never expected to be working together as a mainline freight crew. While we were stopped at Case Siding to make a pick-up in the Rockford yard, Chet and I took pictures of each other on the rear platform of the caboose.

Continuing eastward, we met First 73 (CFS-3) with GP40 3059, which was in Buckbee Siding at Rockford, and met Second 73 (the local) making his pick-up off the EJ&E at Munger with a Katy F-unit set led by my old friend, the 64C. We made pretty good time over the road, but the clock was running out on us by the time we arrived at Markham.

The Federal Hours of Service Law limited us to 16 hours on duty, and we'd already used up about ten. Noting that the units were all facing east, the yardmaster said that he'd probably have to make us lay over for eight hours rest before we could head back west. "By the time you get those units turned on the wye," he said, "you won't have time to get home."

Chet asked if there was any restriction against running the engines long-hood forward. "It's up to the engineer," he was told.

"Hey, Soup," Chet called on the radio. "They'll let us go home if we don't take time to turn the engines. Do you mind running 'em backwards?"

"Heck, I'll run 'em sideways if they'll let us go home," he replied.

I recall that we got our train stuffed into C Yard, snatched our caboose and were ready to go west in 22 minutes. There was some speculation that it was a record performance.

We were lined onto the main line by the Harvey switchtender and caboose-hopped into the night. Because a short train can "phantom" the block signals and not be detected if it moves too fast, two light units are limited to 25 m.p.h., and three units are permitted only 45 m.p.h. in block-signal territory. We were

making the authorized 50-m.p.h. track speed up around Kensington when the dispatcher took exception to our pace and suggested we slow down to the two-unit speed. The fact that we were four units long didn't seem to sink in with him, but we didn't argue. At Hawthorne we picked up 21 cars, making us legal for track speed, and we made an uneventful run for home in the dim light of dawn. It was the only time Chet and I worked together.

George and the Dynamics

Though I didn't flaunt it, my work with EMD had given me a lot of experience around locomotives, and I got to be a pretty good judge of engineers. We had some very good ones, and we had some not-so-good ones. One of the nicest people but one of the worst engineers was George Smith Jr. Word around the railroad was that old George Sr. was probably the worst hoghead to ever beat a 2400 over the road, and that he singlehandedly ruined more firemen than everybody else put together. He thought that the Johnson bar was a three-position toggle— forward, neutral and reverse— and felt that if he wasn't making any noise he wasn't doing any work.

"Junior" was a chip off the old block. I had to carry a broken knuckle only twice during my IC tenure, and George's initials were on both of 'em. But other than that, he was a very easy guy to get along with.

One day we were romping westward with the local out of Markham, which was used to balance motive power and always got a good set of locomotives. This day we had three new GP40's, two empty gondolas, a refrigerator car and a caboose, and were clipping along at about 65 m.p.h. toward Munger where we had to stop and pick up at the EJ&E. There's about a half percent grade westbound through Munger, and I mentioned to George that all of our units were the dynamic-brake-equipped 3060's and maybe he should give 'em a try.

"Oh, them dynamics are no damned good!" he spouted as we crested the hill (which was

CHET FRENCH, the author's long-time friend, was the conductor on the Chain Gang Extra 9513 East, and he posed for this photo in the twilight with the caboose stopped on the main line at Rockford while the head end made its pick-up. This was the only road job the author and Chet worked together.

A TYPICAL Freeport District scene was CC-6 eastbound (top) at Plato Center in September 1970. The Freeport District was faster than the timetable-authorized speed of 60 m.p.h. for freight might suggest, as evidenced (above) by the speedometer reading 69 m.p.h. on 3061 on Second CC-6 on October 9, 1969.

his way of saying "I don't know the first thing about dynamic brakes").

"Sure they are, George. I've seen 'em used a lot on these engines. Just pop the selector into 'D' as you come over the top, ease out to bunch the slack and then wind 'em out."

"Aw, them things ain't worth crap," he shot back, now getting a bit flustered.

"C'mon, George. Give 'em a try," I persisted.

I really had him rattled, for he came over the top of the hill, made a service application on the big air and bailed off the independent. This set up the air brakes on the train and released the brakes on the engines. But our engines outweighed the entire train by a factor of about three to one. Those two empty gons, the freezer and caboose were quickly engulfed in brakeshoe smoke as those three orange lead-sleds hurtled downhill. It was like trying to use a fishing sinker for an anchor to stop a speedboat. George should have known better than to bail that independent.

We hurtled past the Munger depot at a mile a minute with the caboose almost lost in the brakeshoe smoke. George was muttering unprintable things, and I was trying hard to keep from laughing. We finally rolled to a stop at Coleman, on the other side of the Fox River bridge, and George had to explain to the dis-

patcher why he was going to have to back up through a block signal to make the pick-up at Munger. George was rather quiet for the rest of the trip, and I never again brought up the subject of dynamic brakes with him.

"Slick" Slattery

One engineer I didn't get along with at all was "Slick" Slattery. He was a powerfully built middle-age man who looked and dressed like an outlaw biker—complete with black Harley T-shirt and engineer boots. Although I never saw him drunk on duty, Ol' Slick did like his liquid refreshment, and the scariest trip I ever made over the east end was on the local with Slick. We had Geep 8103 with bad springs, and Slick was hammering down through Plato Center at 83 m.p.h. trying to get into Markham before the bars closed. I thought he was going to put us in the ditch and threatened to pull the air if he didn't slow down to at least 70. That really ticked him off, but I wasn't kidding. He slowed down and put me rather high on his list of Least Favorite People.

A few months later in early winter I got called for the Madison Job and found Slick on the engine with Kenny Steele, a tall, soft-talking fireman out of Iaeger, West Virginia. Slick wasn't particularly happy to see me, but I didn't particularly care.

We got our single Paducah Geep off the diesel pit and were rolling down the main line toward the west end of Wallace Yard when Slick erupted loudly. "My God, this engine's not loading!"

"What's the matter?" asked Kenny.

"This thing's not loading. Look, the ammeter's dead. We've gotta' get another engine."

Now, the unit was obviously loading or we wouldn't be making 40 m.p.h., but that bit of logic had somehow escaped our astute throttle jockey. Slick grabbed the radio and reported his "trouble" to the yardmaster, who told him that there were no other units available and he'd have to keep this one.

"But it's not loading," he protested, jerking the throttle back and forth and watching the motionless ammeter but apparently ignoring the fact that the Geep was speeding up and slowing down as he did it.

Finally I couldn't keep quiet any longer. "The No. 2 traction motor is cut out; everything else is okay."

"You're just a damned brakeman; now shut up and sit down," Slick shot back. Then he told Kenny to see what he could do. At Slick's urging, he opened up the electrical cabinet and began poking things with a flagstick.

"Check those fuses!" Slick bellowed.

Getting pretty tired of this, Kenny gave me a wink and followed Slick's instructions to the letter. He grabbed a fuse and gave it a yank. With a brilliant shower of sparks, the Aux Gen fuse came out, cutting off all control power. With the auxiliary generator now incapacitated, the entire control stand went dead, and the diesel engine rumbled to a stop. All you could hear was some heavy breathing and the clickety-clack of our wheels on the rails as we coasted dead into West Junction.

I didn't say a word.

Kenny got the fuse back in and restarted the engine. The Geep That Wouldn't Load eased into the West Yard and coupled onto the Madison train. Kenny was now in the long hood by the starter switch. "While you're back there, check out the traction motor cut-outs," Slick reluctantly suggested.

"Yep, there's one cut out."

"Which one?"

"Number 2."

Slick just glared at me, but I had to stick it to him. "On an EMD engine, the ammeter reads the No. 2 traction motor; cut out No. 2 and you lose the ammeter," I explained.

Slick exploded. "You're just a damned brakeman, and I told you to shut up. Now get the hell offa' my engine and don't come back."

The only one who got the short end of that deal was poor old Pat Corrigan, who was half crippled and could hardly see. The regular rear brakeman on the Madison Job, Pat hadn't done anything but ride the caboose for nearly a decade. As we stopped to line ourselves onto the Madison Branch, I dropped back to the caboose, and Pat went up front to calm down our hoghead. Even though he worked harder that day than he'd done in quite a while, Pat later admitted with a grin that the humor of the situation hadn't escaped him. And it was almost worth it to watch Slattery simmer every time he looked at that dead ammeter.

The Madison Branch

Most of my trips on the Madison Branch were a bit less emotionally charged than the one with Slick Slattery. The picturesque line rambled some 60 miles through the rolling countryside to the Wisconsin state capital. It served a number of cheese factories around Monroe, had its own tunnel and sometimes served as a route for coal headed to the University of Wisconsin power plant. The six-day-a-week Madison Job with one Geep, a dozen or so cars and a caboose was the classic American branchline local, and I always enjoyed working it with regulars like Kenny Anderson,

A wreck on the Rock Island in May 1971 resulted in Rock Island train 6-8 detouring into Chicago on the Santa Fe from Joliet and pulling alongside IC's WC-2 waiting at the 21st Street interlocking. The wayward "*Rocket*" would enter IC tracks at AT&SF Junction (21st Street), follow WC-2 up to the St. Charles Air Line and transfer back to home rails at 16th Street interlocking.

THE MADISON BRANCH was a picturesque line that featured one of the few tunnels on the IC; in January 1971 (above left) **the Madison Job was approaching the south portal, four miles north of Monticello, Wisconsin. In October 1970 the Madison Job was at Exeter crossing just south of the tunnel** (above right) **with one of the Pauley Cheese URTX 36000-series refrigerator cars first out. Wisconsin dairy farms were numerous along the branch where the Madison Job was northbound crossing a timber trestle** (below) **just above Monroe, Wisconsin, on October 14, 1970.**

Pat Corrigan and "Itchy" Dickinson. Like the two long Gruber jobs and the Mendota Turn, the Madison had its own assigned caboose, a modern extended-vision cupola model—all the other trains out of Wallace got pool cabooses.

There were a couple of big cheese factories on the Racine Street Spur on the south side of Monroe that were interesting to switch. And the little Pauley Cheese plant on the north side of the tracks uptown had its own fleet of six assigned refrigerator cars. If one of the handsome orange-with-brown-ends URTX freezers in the 36000 series showed up at Freeport, you didn't need to check the list to know it was destined for Pauley's at Monroe.

Probably the most distinctive feature of the Madison Branch was the tunnel at Milepost 40 between Monticello and Belleville. The 1,280-foot-long rock bore had about two miles of 1 percent climb on either side of it and was on a slight curve. With that bend, you could

lose sight of both ends while in the middle of it, and in the winter it could grow some pretty impressive icicles on the inside.

The Madison Branch was always a welcome call, and one of the most pleasant memories I have of working on the IC was returning from Madison one warm autumn afternoon, riding the rear platform of the cushion-underframe caboose, seated on an overturned milk crate just enjoying the breeze and listening to the clickety-clack of the jointed rail as we rocked through the cornfields at the prescribed 25 m.p.h. pace—and getting paid for it.

Because Wisconsin law still required a fireman on all trains, the position was not optional on the Madison Job. If there was no protected fireman available, the job would be filled by a brakeman off the extra board—and I was lucky enough to catch one such call. Reporting to work, I offered to swap off with one of the old heads on the crew and do the "ground

pounding" for them, but Pat Corrigan told me to stay on the engine and just be a good fireman. That was the one day in my railroading career that I worked in engine service for pay.

Train Orders

The lines out of Freeport were all operated with train orders, and the Waterloo-Chicago main line was also ABS (Automatic Block Signal) territory with—west of Freeport—segments of Centralized Traffic Control. It felt like "real railroading" to get a pink clearance form and a fistful of traditional green Form 19 train orders when you hit the road. Only one time was I involved in a train-order problem.

We were taking the local east out of Wallace one evening as Second Class No. 72. Since eastbounds are superior by direction to westbounds, the eastbounds usually hold the main on a meet. It was shortly after dark, and we had a meet with 73, drag freight CFS-3, at Evarts, ten miles east of Freeport. The block signal at the east end of Evarts was still green as we pulled up on the main line, and I was just about to get down and line the siding for 73 when the conductor radioed from the caboose, "Check your train orders."

We reread the order, "Number 72 take siding at Evarts and meet Number 73."

Oops. There we were naked as a jaybird on the main line. We heard 73 talking as he was coming through Rockford. I reached for the radio to ask the conductor what to do, when the engineer grabbed the mic and gave me a "shush" sign. "Just look back," he said.

There, about 75 carlengths to the west, was a red fusee being swung around in a big back-up sign. Maintaining radio and whistle silence, we eased back to the west end of Evarts and lined the switch just as the signal off to the east dropped red.

"How ya' doin' out there?" called Benny Beirau on 73. "I'm just coming into Steward" (about six miles away).

"We're just headin' in at Evarts, Benny," the conductor replied. "Keep 'em coming; we'll be out of your way in a couple of minutes. You're runnin' a little slow tonight, aren't you, Benny?"

"Nah, the trainmaster was out there at Alworth and pulled a test on us."

The block signals would have prevented a catastrophe, of course, but that would not have covered our *faux pas* to the crew of approaching 73—had they not been delayed by Pete Clayton and the road foreman. The pair had been at the crossing in Alworth, east of us, "pulling a test" on westbound 73 and Benny Beirau (the most safety-conscious engineer on the roster) by planting a red fusee on the track to see if he would stop. Meanwhile, a dozen miles behind Clayton's back, the less astute crew on No. 72 had blown a meet order! Clayton would never know it, but by pulling that test and stalling 73, he'd saved our butts.

BRAKEMAN HOWARD SHEPPARD is standing by the pilot of the southbound Mendota Turn at the south end of the siding at Woosung, Illinois, as northbound 372 out of Clinton holds the main line, on its way home to Freeport.

Crazy Carl

You learn quickly to trust your fellow workers and to work as a team—railroad equipment is big and unforgiving and can kill you. And it can be a dangerous weapon in the wrong hands.

We had one such set of wrong hands working out of Freeport. Engineer Carl Kettlehut was a strange character who thought it was good sport to cause an "incident" in an effort to get somebody else in trouble. He was so good at covering his tracks that nobody could ever prove anything and get him canned, but the trainmasters watched him pretty carefully. Everybody warned me about him, so I wasn't totally unprepared when he tried his little tricks on me.

Carl was the regular engineer on one of the two Gruber road jobs that worked south to Clinton. No one with any seniority would bid the head brakeman's job with Carl, so that side of the Long Gruber always went to the extra board.

Carl lit right into me when I caught my first job with him. He would start talking politics or religion or sex and try to goad you into an argument. Then he'd get nasty and personal, and a lot of guys would really get upset and be ready to fight. I thought his arguments were kind of fun, and I got along with him pretty well by not taking anything seriously and just taking his doses of bullfeathers and giving them back to him double. He seemed to love it. Our across-the-cab "discussions" got pretty outrageous, but it was good sport.

The first time I saw his treacherous side, however, was a bitterly cold winter day as we were doing some work at Dixon. Without warning, Carl shoved the blind end of a cut of cars across the busy Seventh Street crossing, which was unprotected while both the conductor and I were in the yard office. If anything had happened, he could have made it look like it was our fault.

I got an even more personal dose of it a couple of weeks later when we were switching south of Bloomington. We had a couple of boxcars to set out behind about a dozen cars that we were carrying on the head end. Normally we would pull up with me riding the rear car of the cut, and I would drop off to unlock and

remove the derail on the siding, then stop Carl with the radio and walk forward to line the siding switch. This time, however, there was some tangled fencing material in the frozen ditch between the siding and the main, and the icy footing along the siding was very poor.

I stayed on the boxcar and rode it up to the switch, stopped Carl, lined the switch and radioed him: "Back up about four car lengths; the footing here is pretty tricky and I'm going to ride the end car back to the derail. I'll stop you with the radio to unlock the derail."

"Okay, I understand," he replied. That move would have been fine with anybody else, and I didn't realize that I'd just set myself up with Carl. He started shoving backward and was picking up speed. "Easy, Carl . . . that'll do. *That'll do!* Stop, Carl!!"

I bailed off a split second before that big Southern Railway boxcar hit the derail. Since it was the "back side" of the derail, the car lurched upwards, rode over the derail casting, came back down on the track and rebounded toward me. I looked up to see the side of the boxcar filling the whole sky above my head. Then it rocked back upright and settled down, still on the track, as Carl dynamited the air.

"What happened? I didn't hear the radio!" he hollered innocently. I had told him to back up four car lengths to the derail, and he accelerated backward like he was going for four miles. He knew damned well what he was doing, and if I hadn't jumped, I would probably been thrown forty or fifty feet into the air when the boxcar hit that derail. But like always, there was no proof, and he could have made me look like the one who made the mistake if there had been an investigation.

From then on I was always on my guard around Carl. (A few years later, Carl was fired when he ran a "stop and flag" order at the TP&W crossing in El Paso, Illinois, after the home signal had been damaged by a nearby highway accident. Even the engineers' union regarded it as good riddance and wouldn't come to his defense.)

Orton Odyssey

Rrrrrring! My phone came to life at 2 a.m. on Tuesday, Dec. 1, 1970. The caller announced, "Boyd, you're called for a work train for three days on the Gruber. Deadhead to Minonk by car; the conductor's driving and will be leaving Wallace at 4:40."

I asked if I could take my own car, and he said it was okay as long as I got to Minonk to go on duty at 7 a.m. There had been two

IN JANUARY 1971, No. 373, the "Long Gruber" freight from Freeport to Clinton, was stopped at the home signal at Minonk, Illinois, as Santa Fe's Pekin Branch local worked across the diamond.

THE WRECK SCENE at Rutland, Illinois (above)**, consisted of about 15 cars that had been moved off the main line but now needed to be picked up using IC's Orton wrecker and Hulcher's Caterpillars, like the side-boom working the end of the boxcar. One of the wrecking-crew workers** (far left) **presented an amazing appearance after slinging cables underneath a loaded hopper that was leaking carbon black. Cook Paul Kraft** (left) **had the table set for lunch in the heavyweight diner.**

wrecks in the past couple of weeks, and we were to pick up the damaged equipment at Minonk and Rutland that had been pushed aside to clear the track, which had been rebuilt and opened for service. Our work train, the Waterloo wrecker, had been relayed south on the local and the La Salle switcher and was now at Minonk—or so we were told.

One hundred and ten miles later at 6:50 a.m., I was driving around Minonk looking at a very barren railroad. The section foreman told me that the work train was nine miles back north at Wenona! I was relieved to find that our engineer, Ernie Batalia, had made the same mistake and was just checking out the locomotive when I arrived.

We put our train together with black Geep 9381, the 160-ton Orton diesel wrecking crane X-110, a boom tender, a panel-track rack car, an outfit diner, an outfit Pullman, a tool car, about 20 gons and flats and a ca-

boose. Then we headed south for Minonk.

The wreck was a small one involving four cars, with only one remaining for us to pick up. We dropped off the outfit cars, spotted the Orton at the derailed car, pulled the engine into the clear and went to breakfast. When we returned 40 minutes later, the derailed carbon black covered hopper was already on the track on its own trucks. One down.

A "DOME HITCH" was used to lift two derailed tank cars at the Rutland wreck site. Like a giant T-bar cuff-link, the inverted "T" with a pilot at the cross was lowered into the tank car dome and the swung out inside the car. The entire car was then simply lifted by the dome and swung over into a gondola. It was neat and quick.

As a brakeman, my job in all of this was to stay with the locomotive and handle any switching that was needed. The wreck train had its own crew of specialists to rerail or salvage the damaged cars.

We got everything together and shoved about five miles north to Rutland where the real mess was. Chet French later told me that brakeman Gary Carr had been riding in the caboose with conductor Freddy Carrithers when he saw the freight cars ahead of him start to fly. "I just saw a car go straight up in the air!" he shouted incredulously to Fred.

The conductor simply replied, "Hang on."

About 15 cars had stacked up in the middle of town when another hopper had rocked itself off the track (the same thing that had happened at Minonk). Cars were scattered on both sides of the main line, but the track was clear. We shoved the Orton and outfit cars

onto the grain-elevator track and got the empty gons and flats next to the engine.

The Orton was put into gear, and it moved itself to the derailment site. It laboriously positioned itself for the first lift and cranked out the outriggers as workers built up timber blocking for the outriggers to rest on. It seemed to be a cumbersome and time-consuming process.

Enter the whiz-bangers! With a sudden flurry of activity from the nearby highway, a caravan of trucks burst upon the scene. The M. L. Hulcher Emergency Service Company is an outfit that you have to see in action to believe. With a huge D-8 Caterpillar bulldozer and a Cat 580 side-boom, they tore into that wreck like buzzards on a road kill. A side-boom is a heavy Caterpillar dozer with a stiff-leg wrecking boom on its right side balanced by a heavy counterweight that can be swung far out on the left side. It's an amazing piece of machinery to watch.

With winches at their drawbars, two Cats tied onto a boxcar and dragged it over beside the track while the Orton was still deploying its outriggers. The Orton grabbed one end of the boxcar while the side-boom positioned two freight trucks on the track and then ran around and grabbed the other end of the boxcar. Together they lifted the boxcar straight up and swung it over the trucks. In a few minutes it was back on the track and ready to roll.

Then the Orton tucked in its outriggers and backed itself onto the elevator track while we pulled up with the locomotive and moved the boxcar out of the way. Meanwhile the side-boom and dozer were growling around getting the next car into position. The Orton then

HEADED NORTH just below La Salle, Illinois, the "hospital train" was headed home with the wrecker outfit up front and the crippled wrecks being nursed along behind. The job wasn't done, however, because just as this picture was being taken, 30 miles to the north Buck Woods was dumping two boxcars and four cob gons of the Mendota Turn on the ground. Tomorrow would be another work day for the wrecker crew.

repositioned and deployed its outriggers for the next lift.

The pattern repeated itself for nearly every car. Between Hulcher and our Orton, within half a day we had all but four cars picked up and back on their trucks or stowed on flatcars. Whatever IC paid Hulcher for its services, it must have been worth it in the time saved.

There's more to a wreck train than a big hook, however, and one of the more delightful traditions is the outfit diner. Our car was a standard heavyweight, only slightly modified from its revenue-service days. The hospitable cook, Paul Kraft from Waterloo, saw that the train and wrecking crews were fed. He set a hearty meal with huge quantities of meat, potatoes, vegetables and all the trimmin's.

Of course, that first evening meal was not without incident. This was Paul's first trip as a dining-car cook, and while he was preparing dinner, we had to shove the outfit cars with us up to Wenona to get rid of the re-railed cripples. A 20 m.p.h. gait on the Gruber's track was not conducive to passenger equipment travel, and suddenly the ham was 'twixt the apple pie while fried chicken grease was splattered onto the stove—and the whole pan caught fire! Paul quickly pitched the pyrotechnic provisions out the door and almost set a right-of-way fire. He was seen from the caboose standing in the dining-car door shaking a meat cleaver at the engineer.

Since there was no hotel nearby, I was invited by one of the wreck crew to spend the night in the outfit bunk car. Bunk car? It was an almost untouched eight-section, one-drawing-room, three-double-bedroom heavyweight Pullman sleeper with rooms and berths intact and in use (cars of this type were used on the *Seminole* and *Louisiane*). That night I slept in a Pullman car on the grain elevator track in beautiful downtown Rutland, Illinois. How about that for a "rare mileage" fantrip?

The next morning we were back to work cleaning up the rest of the Rutland wreck. The wreck was completely cleared by noon, and we got the train together and headed north with 29 cars, including the outfit cars and cripples. The conductor and I drove our cars beside the train, keeping an eye on everything with numerous slow runby inspections. Nearing La Salle, I went ahead with the conductor to check our train orders at the depot. As we stepped into the office, Bob Burris, a brakeman on the La Salle switcher greeted us, "Buck Woods just put 'em in the ditch at Sublette; you're not going home tonight!"

We spent the next day picking up two boxcars and four gondolas full of corn cobs that had been dumped by the Mendota Turn. If you have to get stuck behind a derailment, it's nice to have a wrecking crane with you—and Hulcher's phone number.

"Just Stop Everything!"

Derailments are potentially dangerous mishaps, of course, but I do recall one that had (to me, anyway) a humorous side. I was working head end on CAC-5 from Chicago to Freeport, and as we were easing in for the stop on the Westbound Main at Wallace Yard, I noticed a pile of tank cars on the east end of the West Yard. I was the first one into the yard office and casually commented to the yardmaster (an extra man who was a miserable cuss to work with), "That's quite a little mess you've got there in the West Yard, isn't it, Joe?"

"What mess?" he shot back with just a touch of alarm in his voice.

"That pile of tank cars out there."

"Pile of tank cars . . . *Omigod!*" He grabbed the radio and shouted, "West Job, stop what you're doing right now! Just stop everything!"

It seems that something had come off the track near the east end of the West Yard, and the midnight switch crew—unaware of the problem—had just been banging Apple River empties into that dark track all night, adding to the pile with every kick. Fortunately, nobody was hurt—and the look on Joe's face when he saw those tank cars was worth a lot of long hours putting up with him on the midnight job.

Amtrak Arrives

By the spring of 1971 we knew changes were in the works for IC and railroads in general with the coming of the National Railroad Passenger Corporation: Amtrak. Start-up was set for May 1, and as that date neared, I took every opportunity to photograph passenger trains in and around Chicago, including the *Hawkeye* at Freeport and Rockford.

The final week of April brought railfan activity almost to a fever pitch as we plotted ways to photograph the most-inconvenient and elusive of the area's trains that had been overlooked in the past. Helping out in this historic endeavor was the fact that, due to some vacations being taken, the Rockford night switch engine had an open job which nobody seemed to want. So for my first time on the IC, I bid on a job and was able to hold it for two weeks. With a regular work schedule, I could make railfan trips to Chicago without having to worry about missing an extra board call—and the Rockford job had a convenient schedule, going to work at 10:30 p.m. and getting off duty at 6:30 a.m. I could hop into Chicago, take pictures all day, drive back to Rockford, grab a nap in my car and go to work that night. You didn't want to try that stunt two days in a row, but once or twice a week with a good day's rest in between wasn't too bad.

Rockford was an interesting job to work because the yard was rather unusual: The ladder tracks ran uphill. Most yards, like Wallace, were "dish" shaped, with the tracks dropping gently downhill to the center. That way you could "kick" cars without using air brakes, and they would sooner or later settle themselves in the middle of the dish.

Since switching a yard using air brakes is very time-consuming, they had worked out a unique system for "kick switching" Rockford. While the conductor lined the switches, one brakeman would "pull the pins" to uncouple the cars while the "field man" would stay up in the ladder tracks with wooden blocks to "scotch" each car as it rolled to a stop to prevent it from rolling back downhill toward the lead where the train was working. If a car crushed the block and began to roll, the field man would have to climb aboard and stop it with the hand brake. Every once in a while more than one track at a time would start to roll, and the whole crew would be madly dashing around the yard with scotch blocks and grabbing for handbrakes.

The Rockford job was unusual in another aspect. There was some industrial trackage on the east side of town that was shared by IC, Milwaukee and Burlington, and each year the Quaker Oats switching would rotate among the three roads. It happened that IC had the job in spring '71, and we needed to be over there about 1 a.m. to spot empties for loading.

"Quaker Oats" was a rather polite name for what was really a slaughterhouse that produced dogfood. Other than a few inbound covered hoppers of grain, the Quaker business was primarily outbound "RBL" insulated boxcars of canned dogfood.

We would often spot the cars at Quaker and then go "on the spot" ourselves for a couple of hours while they were being loaded. On more than one occasion while photographing the

AMTRAK ARRIVED on May 1, 1971, and a gaggle of fans was on hand at Rockford at 6:30 a.m. to watch the last *Hawkeye*, No.12, which would complete its trip to Chicago after having begun its run in Sioux City before midnight. Amtrak initially kept IC equipment and power on the *City of New Orleans*; on August 29, 1971, the *City* was awaiting departure from Central Station (right) **alongside the Seaboard Coast Line power that would handle the Amtrak *South Wind*, which had in essence replaced IC's *City of Miami*.**

last passenger trains before May 1, that hour or so of spot time at Quaker was the only sleep I'd get in 24 hours.

You never got an early quit on the Rockford job, because the agent, Bill Groves, would get out around 5 a.m. to see if there was any last-minute work he could give the switch crew before they went off duty at 6:30. On the Saturday morning of May 1, 1971, however, he let the switch crew go home a half hour early because he knew I wanted to photograph the last eastbound *Hawkeye* at Rockford at 6:30.

So did he.

I'd been in Chicago all day Friday, April 30, photographing last outbound departures and inbound arrivals of those trains that would be killed by Amtrak. IC's last pair of E6's had gone out in style, back-to-back on the final *Governor's Special* to Springfield. Among other trains, I'd photographed the last outbound *City of Miami* and had gotten the last westbound *Hawkeye* at dusk at 21st Street.

After getting off work to photograph the last inbound *Hawkeye* on Saturday morning, I headed into Chicago to photograph more arrivals of trains that had begun their journeys before midnight and the first runs of Amtrak-operated trains. Most Amtrak operations were

concentrated at Chicago's Union Station, but a few Amtrak trains continued to use Central Station. However, the scene was already changing there, too.

Amtrak wanted only stainless-steel equipment, so the IC's *Panama*-scheme fleet of streamlined smooth-sides was doomed. The first resurrected *South Wind* out of Central Station on the morning of May 1 made that message clear: Shiny Louisville & Nashville E-units led all-stainless-steel consist.

In the weeks and months that followed, IC equipment was included in some bizarre sights, like a mostly stainless-steel *City of New Orleans* departing Chicago. Amtrak had acquired a number of IC's best E-units, but the orange-and-brown smooth-side cars that could still be seen here and there were only being leased and were living on borrowed time.

For us on the Freeport District, Amtrak simply meant two less jobs.

The Dixon Job

Back when I was in high school, I used to hang around the Seventh Street crossing and listen to Louie Scott laying out the day's work to Govie Bates and Jack Taylor. "We'll build the Medusas on the North House, line up the

NORTHBOUND 372 out of Clinton was crossing the Rock River trestle at Dixon in August 1970 and was viewed from the riverbank in front of Dixon High School. The tall stacks are on the Commonwealth Edison coal-fired power plant, the old "INU" facility that used to receive trainloads of coal in the huge C&IM gondolas, which were unloaded by cranes with clamshells—no rotary dumper here.

CENTENNIAL "MARKERS" featuring 11-inch bronze medallions on 1,500-pound limestone blocks, slabs or mahogany panels were presented to 150 locations on the IC during its 100th birthday celebration in 1951. Dixon's marker was on the northeast side of the Seventh Street crossing, where No. 373 was headed for Clinton in March 1970.—MIKE MCBRIDE

INUs on the South Middle and put the Bordens on the South House . . . "

It sounded like so much gobbledygook to me back then, but I was fascinated, even though "switching" seemed like such a pointless exercise in going back and forth. Besides, when all of that was done, maybe there'd be a caboose ride down to River Street.

Now here I was at age 29, standing at Seventh Street with a switch list in my hand while conductor Jack Taylor was telling me that we'd ". . . build the Medusas on the North House, line up the INUs on the South Middle and put the Bordens on the South House . . ."

But now it all made sense.

I got called for the Dixon Job about a half dozen times, and it was always a special treat to work the hometown switcher as a legitimate part of the crew. As a railfan working for

EMD and schmoozing a cab ride here and there, I'd always felt like an outsider. But working on the IC, I belonged. And nowhere did I belong more than on the Dixon Job.

Bob Morgridge's Whistle

Back in the mid-1960's Chet French had discovered that GP7 8950 had a rather special air horn. Delivered in November 1950, the 8950 was one of IC's first two Geeps, and it had a "modulating" whistle valve in the cab. Whereas the conventional IC valves were either "on" or "off," giving sharp-edged blasts on the air horns, the modulating valve would let the engineer "quill" the air horn like a steam whistle, trailing it off gracefully.

One day I was southbound on Gruber freight 373 with the 7950, the Paducah-rebuilt 8950, which had retained its modulating whistle valve through the conversion. Our engineer was Bob Morgridge, a very pleasant individual and a gentleman in every sense of the word. I knew that he'd been on the Gruber in steam and then had gone into Chicago to take up various supervisory jobs before returning to Freeport to work his last years before retirement as an engineer again.

Approaching Dixon, Bob noticed that "different" whistle valve. Drifting downhill on the north side, he began to play with the valve—suddenly I was listening to a sound that I hadn't heard since before the end of steam!

Bob was stringing those seven crossings together, trailing off each two-longs-a-short-and-a-long but never quite letting it die before bringing in the next one. I just stared across the cab as we rolled over Squires Avenue and I could see my old home framed in the cab window behind Bob's silhouette.

"Hey, Bob," I asked, "what year did you leave the Gruber and take that fuel supervisor's job in Chicago?"

"About 1952, as I recall," he replied.

"Did you whistle like that on the steam engines coming through here?"

"I sure did. There was nothing prettier than stringing those North Dixon crossings together on the steamboat whistle of a 2100."

"You know where I used to live up beyond

Squires Avenue when I was a kid, don't you? Well, I used to lay awake at night hoping that a train coming down the hill would blow the whistle like that. It was the prettiest thing I'd ever heard. The last time I remember hearing it was about three years before the end of steam, around 1952."

That big guy just looked at me and was almost too choked up to speak. The whistle artist finally knew that somebody out there had been paying attention. ◆

THE DIXON JOB was spotting a car at the Dixon Publishing siding (above) on the River Track as it passed behind a house on Sixth Street in July 1971. The author took his last IC photo (below) in July 1972 as No. 373 ducked under the Bloody Gulch Road bridge south of Dixon. After this, it was Illinois Central Gulf.

CHAPTER 7

Working out of Freeport in the early summer of 1971, I was aware that I was living the last of the steam era. Here was a railroad that still rostered its first road freight diesel (GP7 8950), had five-man crews complete with firemen, regularly set out 40-foot boxcars at grain elevators and carried cabooses on the end of its Form 19-dispatched trains. And there were veteran steam engineers like Bob Morgridge who knew that the whistle cord could be something more than a utilitarian safety appliance.

It was too good to last.

The first shock wave of tomorrow's railroading hit me right in the paycheck. The national labor agreements had expired, and the railroads and the unions hadn't agreed on new ones. The railroads wanted to end the traditional 100-mile crew districts and eliminate firemen and extra brakemen. The unions, of course, were fiercely resisting. We were working under the old agreements as negotiations continued. On July 16, 1971, the United Transportation Union went on strike against the Southern Railway and Union Pacific, and in retaliation the non-struck railroads instituted sweeping work-rules revisions. The strike hit the IC on July 25 and lasted until early August. When it was over, the steam era was gone forever, and the union had given up a lot of traditional work rules for a 42 percent wage increase over the next 42 months. It was something that had to happen and would mean survival for the entire industry in the decades to come—and it changed my life directly.

It took a while for the effect to be felt at Wallace. Following the strike, I caught yard jobs on August 4th and 5th, a long Gruber on the 8th, two more Wallace switch engines on the 11th and 12th, a Chain Gang Extra to Chicago on the 15th (page 99) and the local into Markham on the 18th.

Then the new work rules went into effect, cutting a number of jobs, and they immediately set up a "seniority extra board," which meant that after working a job, a man went back on the board in the order of his seniority rather than at the end of the list. Thus, the senior men got all the work and the junior men starved. Local No. 91 out of Markham at 6:30 p.m. on July 19, 1971, with Geep 8031 in the lead was my last paid trip on the railroad—134 miles at the local freight rate. Conductor Norm McMurray signed us off at Wallace at 1:30 a.m. on July 20, and I never got another call to work. I sat for a while on that seniority extra board before sanity returned, and they cut six men and returned to a normal extra board. I was one of the six transferred to the "reserve board." I was not fired and maintained seniority, but I would not be called to work. The last paycheck for "J. A. Boyd 34112," for $204.89, was dated August 22, 1971. That was to be, as they say, "the first day of the rest of my life."

Knowing this could last quite a while, I took a job in the camera department of the Giant discount store in Rockford where my railfan friend Stan Guyer worked part time. The work was easy, but the pay wasn't anywhere near what I'd been making on the railroad. I needed a "real" job.

I'd been writing magazine articles for *Railroad Model Craftsman* since the early 1960's, and when I was working for EMD I'd told Tony

THE ILLINOIS CENTRAL GULF merger was evident in July 1974 as GM&O F3 880-B idled outside the running-service building at Woodcrest, and orange ICG Geeps wearing the new "I-ball" herald posed on the ready tracks in the distance.

120

A CLASSIC GM&O image was created in June 1965 at Venice, Illinois, as a two-unit set of F3's pulled up beside a set of GP30's. Since the IC and GM&O numbering systems had few overlaps, ICG did not find it necessary to "vandalize" its own units by hastily renumbering or doing a "black patch" repainting of its units, and most lasted in untouched IC or GM&O livery until they came due for a full repaint.

Koester of the Nickel Plate Historical & Technical Society that publisher Hal Carstens might be needing an editor. Shortly thereafter, Tony went to work for *RMC*, and I started sending my articles to him. Then Tony wanted me to join him at Carstens, but between EMD and the IC, I had no particular desire or need to go. When I got cut off the IC, however, an editor's job in New Jersey sounded pretty good.

Tony prodded Hal, and in September I went east for a job interview. On October 1, 1971, I went to work as the new associate editor of *Flying Models Magazine*, which needed help far more than *RMC* did at that time. I waited until I was firmly established in New Jersey before I resigned from the Illinois Central in November. I would have been called back to work at Wallace about two months later had I not resigned.

When I left the Midwest, the home road was still the Illinois Central, and my break from the past was clean. I now went to sleep in my apartment in Mahwah, New Jersey, with the sound of Erie Lackawanna's former Erie main line only a couple of blocks away. Penn Central was a dirty word, but EL was an accepted merger (from 1960), while Lehigh Valley, Jersey Central, Reading and Lehigh & Hudson River were local favorites. The mention of "Illinois Central" at slide shows got you strange looks. This wasn't the first time I'd been away from the Midwest, and I was too busy exploring my new turf to be homesick. Besides, back home things were changing fast.

The Merger

The long-threatened merger with the Gulf, Mobile & Ohio came on August 10, 1972, creating the Illinois Central Gulf. It sounded like an oil company: "Illinois Central Gulf: Progress Through Petroleum."

GM&O had been a colorful and interesting railroad, and you'd think that the combination of IC and GM&O would produce another strong and viable carrier like Erie Lackawanna—trim some duplicate track and facilities and adopt a bold but traditional image. There was little doubt that IC would dominate the new ICG, as the orange and white was retained with the split-rail herald being only slightly modified into ICG's new version of the "I-Ball." For the first few years things didn't look too bad.

Weirdness

I thought I'd seen some strange sights with Katy F-units and UP DL640's on the IC, but the merger produced some stuff that was downright bizarre. GM&O F-units were repainted into the IC orange and white and demonstrated beyond the shadow of a doubt that nobody had ever thought about how that livery would look on anything other than a hood unit (we'd always wondered if IC would apply the orange and white to the *Panama*-scheme E-units—and supposedly management considered this—but we were mercifully spared the experience). And although I'd seen Alco RS2's in the green diamond black, the

sight of re-engined RS1's in orange and white was quite a shock—almost as much as ICG GP30's and GP35's on Alco trucks.

Like the IC, the new ICG indulged in some interesting leasing arrangements when motive power got tight. It continued the seasonal leasing of Duluth, Missabe & Iron Range SD9's and Bangor & Aroostook's well-maintained GP9's (referred to around Freeport as "them Bangkok & Maines"). The ICG also often operated units like green Reading Geeps and black P&LE's that were awaiting rebuild in the Paducah Shops. And the PECO F-units were replaced by a fleet of Paducah-rebuilt Geeps in the IC paint scheme rendered in Precision National's bright yellow and green.

One thing has to be said for the ICG, however: Unlike the Burlington Northern of the same era, which stripped the heralds and names off its predecessor liveries before repainting, ICG never felt compelled to vandalize its units in the name of merger.

Units stayed for years in virgin GM&O or IC livery until they were completely repainted ICG.

The real enemy was dirt. As maintenance was cut back, the short "shelf life" of the orange and white was becoming very evident, and the vibrant pumpkins of the late 1960's were now giving way to dirty and faded leprosy-liners of the 1970's. The ICG was not doing well, and its motive power showed it.

It was a good time to be living in Jersey.

THE ICG MERGER produced some pretty amazing sights for veteran IC fans, as the orange and white was applied to such unthinkable units as EMD-re-engined RS1's and road-weary F3's. As if to symbolize the "Progress Through Petroleum" image of the ICG name, ex-GM&O RS1m 1133 (left) was switching tank cars at the old GM&O Glenn Yard in Chicago in July 1974. One of the few F-units to get the ICG orange livery, ex-GM&O 809-A, now ICG 1610 (above), was at Bloomington, Illinois, in July 1976. The ICG also leased numerous units including the Bangor & Aroostook GP9's like the 80 at Dixon (below) in December 1973.
—MIKE McBRIDE

ILLINOIS CENTRAL ultimately acquired both the first SD45 and first GP40 produced by EMD. Prototype SD45 4351 became IC 7000 in January 1971, and in August 1974 (top) **it was photographed at Corinth, Mississippi. Black GP40 prototype 433A became IC 3075 in November 1970 but continued to be used by EMD in test sets like the one at Woodcrest** (above) **in June 1971.**

The 7000 and Company

In 1974 I made a trip into the Kentucky coalfields to chase down the last of the IC's—sorry, ICG's—Alco C636's, and in addition to the 1100's, I finally caught the elusive SD45 7000 on a train stopped in the sunshine just outside Corinth, Mississippi. As I was taking its picture, the engineer motioned me up to the cab. "Don't you work for EMD?" he asked. He looked vaguely familiar, and I told him that I used to work for EMD.

"Aren't you the guy who was with me the night we had that dead 6000 in the lead over Adamsville Mountain, and you were giving me amp readings over the radio from the second unit?"

It is definitely a small world.

The 7000 was the very first SD45, EMD demonstrator 4351, and on its debut venture outside of the LaGrange factory, it went testing on the Chicago Great Western in March 1966 in the company of the Santa Fe blue-and-yellow 434 (the prototype SD40 built on an SD35 frame) and the black 433A (my old friend, the prototype GP40 with flared radiator housings). Thanks to the merger, all three units of that 1966 test set ended up on the ICG roster: the 4351 was IC 7000, the 433A was IC 3075, and the 434 was GM&O 950.

On that trip to Kentucky in 1974 I also found the remains of the wreck-damaged 3075 on a flatcar outside the Paducah shop, never to run again. The 7000 lasted until 1987, when it was scrapped. The 950 was still running in the 1990's as IC 6071.

All around the wrecked 3075 in the Paducah boneyard were the battered hulks of the remaining orange-and-brown E-units, displaced by Amtrak and now just fading memories.

Old Flames with New Names

The Illinois Central Gulf would go down in history as one of America's more chaotic mergers—and one that progressed from bad to worse. From its onset in 1972, the merger included not only IC and GM&O but Columbus & Greenville; Fernwood, Columbia & Gulf and Bonhomie & Hattiesburg Southern. The entire 9,400-mile system was one massive network of duplicating trackage whose only hope for suc-

Illlinois Central Final Diesel Roster
March 1929-October 1972

Final IC No.	Original IC No.	Renumber	Builder	Model	H.P.	Date	Notes
200	9300	1200	EMD	SW7	1200	2/50	First Paducah rebuild, 5/67
236	See Note	—	EMD	SW9	1200	1/51	Louisiana Midland 10, acq. with LM 4/67, rebuilt 11/67
400-429	9400-9429	See Notes	EMD	SW7	1200	4-12/50	425 rebuilt as 325 7/67, 419 rebuilt as 1246 12/69, 415 rebuilt as 1303 6/72
430-484	9430-9484	See Notes	EMD	SW9	1200	6/51-6/52	479 rebuilt as 379 8/67; 446, 432, 449, 435, 446, 447 rebuilt as 1244, 1245, 1247-1250 12/69
600-602, BU1	9014-9017	—	EMC	SW1	600	12/39	9017 rebuilt into slug BU1 10/52
603-617	9018-9032	—	EMC/EMD	SW1	600	1/40-8/51	All except 606-608, 611, 612 and 617 retired
—	701	See Notes	Alco	RS2	1500	4/49	Built StL&BE 700, then Peabody Short Line 701, acq. by IC 8/61, retired 2/67
—	702-703	See Notes	Alco	RS2	1500	3/48	Built as Union RR 601-602, then PSL 702-703, acq. by IC 8/61, retired 2/67
800-801	See Notes	—	EMD	SW8	800	11/52	Tremont & Gulf 75, 77, acquired with T&G 8/59
802	See Notes	—	EMD	SW8	800	1/53	Originally CSS&SB 12, then Louisiana Midland 12, acquired with LM 4/67
1000-1016	9150-9166	—	EMC/EMD	NW2	1000	12/39-11/45	1006 sold 5/69, 1009 rebuilt 12/71 as 1301
—	1028A-B	9206A-B	EMD	TR2	1000	11/45	Re# 7/56, retired 2/67
—	1029A-B,1030A-B	9207A-B, 9208A-B	EMD	TR2	1000	12/49	Re# 7/56, 1029A-B rebuilt EMD 10/57, 1030A-B retired 2/67
1075	9205A	9375	EMC	TR	1000	11/40	Cow & calf NW2 cab, rebuilt by EMD as NW2 9375 11/54, re# 1075 9/57 (see also 1235)
1100-1105	—	—	Alco	C636	3600	5/68	Hi-adhesion trucks
1201	9301	—	EMD	SW7	1200	2/50	—
1202-1219	9302-9319	—	EMD	SW7	1200	4-10/50	1217 sold 1/69
1220-1234	9320-9334	—	EMD	SW9	1200	10-11/52	1224 retired 5/68 and converted to truck transfer car
1235	9205B	9335	EMC	TR	1000	11/40	Cow & calf NW2 booster, rebuilt by EMD as SW9 cab 9335 11/54, re# 1235 9/57
1237-1243	See Notes	—	EMD	SW9	1200	4-5/53	Mississippi Central 201-210 acq.with MSC 4/67; 204, 208 sold; 210 leased 4/67
See Notes	—	1244-1250	EMD	SW7/9	1200	8/50-5/52	Rebuild 12/69-5/70 of SW9s 446, 432; SW7 419; SW9s 449, 435, 466 and 449
1300, 1302	9203A, 9204A	1026A, 1027A	EMC	TR	1000	2/40	Cow & calf NW2 cabs, rebuilt and re# 10/71, 4/72
1300B, 1301B	9203B, 9204B	1026B, 1027B	EMC	TR	1000	2/40	Cow & calf NW2 boosters, rebuilt and re# 3/72, 5/72
2021, 2022, 2024	4029, 4030, 4032	—	EMD	E8A	2250	5/32-4/53	Paducah rebuilds 2021, 2/69; 2022, 9/67; 2024, 7/68; 2022 retired 11/69
2036-2040	—	—	EMD	E9A	2400	1/55	Florida East Coast 1031-1035, acquired 5-11/69, not rebuilt by Paducah
2100	4104	—	EMD	E8B	2250	5/52	Rebuilt 2/68, horsepower upped to 2400
3000-3059	—	—	EMD	GP40	3000	2/66-8/69	3057 wrecked 1/69 and rebuilt by EMD with dynamic brakes and 60:17 gearing
3060-3069	—	—	EMD	GP40	3000	8/69	Dynamic brakes, Gyralites and 60:17 gearing
3070-3074	—	—	EMD	GP40	3000	2/70	Dynamic brakes, Gyralites and 60:17 gearing
3075	—	—	EMD	GP40X	3000	5/65	Prototype GP40 EMD 433A acq. 11/70, dynamic brakes,60:17 gearing
—	4000	—	EMC	E6A	2000	10/40	Rebuilt by EMD 8/47 as E7A 4000 7/54
4001-4004	4001-4004	4001A-B, 4002A-B	EMD	E6A	2000	11/41	Re# "A-B" 6/42, re# 4001-4 ?/46, E6 4004 retired 5/54, 4002 5/61, 4003 9/71
—	4000	4004	EMD	E7A	2000	8/47	Rebuild of E6A 4000, re# 4004 7/54, wrecked & retired 1/69
4005-4017	—	—	EMD	E7A	2000	9/46-6/48	4015 wrecked 1/69; 4006, 7, 9 12 retired 5/69; 4016 ret. 1/71; 4017 3/71
4018-4028	—	—	EMD	E8A	2250	6/50-4/52	4019 wrecked 1/70; 4025 retired 1/71, 4026 3/71
4031, 4033	—	—	EMD	E8A	2250	6/52, 4/53	4031 wrecked 6/71, later sceapped; 4032 rebuilt as 2024 7/68
4034-4043	—	—	EMD	E9A	2400	4/54-5/61	4043 wrecked 6/71, later scrapped
4100-4103	—	—	EMD	E7B	2000	9/46-6/48	Traded to EMD 9/56-11/57 for E9B's 4106-4109
4105	—	—	EMD	E8B	2250	5/52	—
4106-4109	—	—	EMD	E9B	2400	9/56-10/57	4109 wrecked 6/71, later scrapped
5000-5005	—	—	GE	U30B	3000	2-3/67	—
5050-5059	—	—	GE	U33C	3300	4-5/68	5055 wrecked & retired 9/69
6000-6005	—	—	EMD	SD40	3000	5/68	No dynamic brakes
6006-6018	—	—	EMD	SD40A	3000	8/69	Dynamic brakes, Gyralites and 60:17 gearing
6019-6023	—	—	EMD	SD40A	3000	1/70	Dynamic brakes, Gyralites and 60:17 gearing
7000	—	—	EMD	SD45	3600	12/65	Prototype SD45 EMD 4351, acquired 1/71
7851	8851	—	EMD	GP7	1500	11/52	Dual controls, later removed
7950	8950	—	EMD	GP7	1500	11/50	IC's first Geep, 8950 b/n 12257
7953-7981	8953-8981	—	EMD	GP7	1500	4/52-4/53	Paducah rebuilds since 1967; 7960 retained high short hood
8000-8041	9000-9041	—	EMD	GP9	1750	4-6/54	9016 chopped but not rebuilt; 8009, 8025 high short hood
8042-8047	9042-9047	—	EMD	GP9	1750	5/54	Built with steam generators, later removed
8048-8199	9048-9199	—	EMD	GP9	1750	12/54-1/57	8082 and 8109 rebuilt with high short hood; 8109 first Paducah Geep rebuild
8204-8219	9204-9219	—	EMD	GP9	1750	1/57	Built with steam generators, removed when rebuilt
8220-8257	9220-9257	—	EMD	GP9	1750	1/57	Not all units rebuilt before ICG merger 8/10/72
8258-8260, 8266-8286	—	—	Paducah	GP10	1850	9/70-9/72	Paducah rebuilds of GP7/9's from IC, SP. FEC, DT&I and QNS&L
8269	8801	—	EMD	GP7	1500	3/53	Dual controls, steam generator, later removed
8300-8389	9300-9389	—	EMD	GP9	1750	12/57-12/58	Paducah rebuilds
8390	—	—	EMD	GP18	1800	2/60	High short hood, GTW 4705, acquired 5/72
8800	—	—	EMD	GP7	1500	1/52	Dual controls, steam generator
8850	—	—	EMD	GP7	1500	11/52	Dual controls
8900, 8901	—	—	EMD	GP7	1500	11/50, 5/51	Steam generator, later removed; 8900 b/n 12258
8902-8911	—	—	EMD	GP7	1500	3-4/53	Steam generator, later removed, 8908 wrecked 6/69, 8909 rebuilt as 7909 10/71
—	8951	—	EMD	GP7	1500	3/51	Sold 12/64 to Meridian & Bigbee as 103
8952	—	—	EMD	GP7	1500	3/51	Equipped as master for slug BU1 at Markham Yard
—	9000-9005	—	GE-IR	Boxcab	600	3/29-2/30	All retired 1950
—	9006-9013	—	Alco	HH660	600	6/35	All retired 1951
—	9200	—	GE-IR	Boxcab	1800	2/36	C-C boxcab powered by 2 IR engines, retired 6/47
—	9201	9202	EMC-StL	Model T	1800	5/36	B-B-B-B steeple cab powered by 2 Winton 201A engines, retired 5/47
—	9202	9201	GE-BS	Boxcab	2000	9/35	First C-C built in U.S., boxcab powered by 2 Busch-Sulzer engines, retired 5/47
9200-9203	—	—	EMD	GP9	1750	1/57	Steam generators, 83 m.p.h. gearing
—	9250A-9250B	1350A-B, 1351A-B	EMD	TR1	1350	4-5/41	Cow & calf transfer units on Blomberg trucks, re# 7/56, retired 2/67
—	9275	400	GE	44-ton	380	11/47	Re# 400 8/56, re# 200 12/59, sold 10/61
9400-9414	—	—	EMD	GP18	1800	3/60	High short hood
9415-9428	—	—	EMD	GP18	1800	3-11/63	Low short hood
9429-9440	—	—	EMD	GP28	1800	3-12/64	Low short hood
9441	—	—	EMD	GP28	1800	9/64	Mississippi Central 211, acquired with MSC 4/67
9500-9519	—	—	EMD	GP38AC	2000	2/70	Dynamic brakes and Gyralites

NOTE: Not all GP7/9's in the 7902-7981 and 8000-8339 groups were rebuilt and renumbered by the 8/10/72 ICG merger, and some were rebuilt as 8000-8300 series GP10s. For complete rebuild dates and numbers, see Extra 2200 South Issue 93 (Oct.-Dec. 1991). **Roster compiled** by Jim Boyd from *Extra 2200 South*, Lee Hastman and other sources.

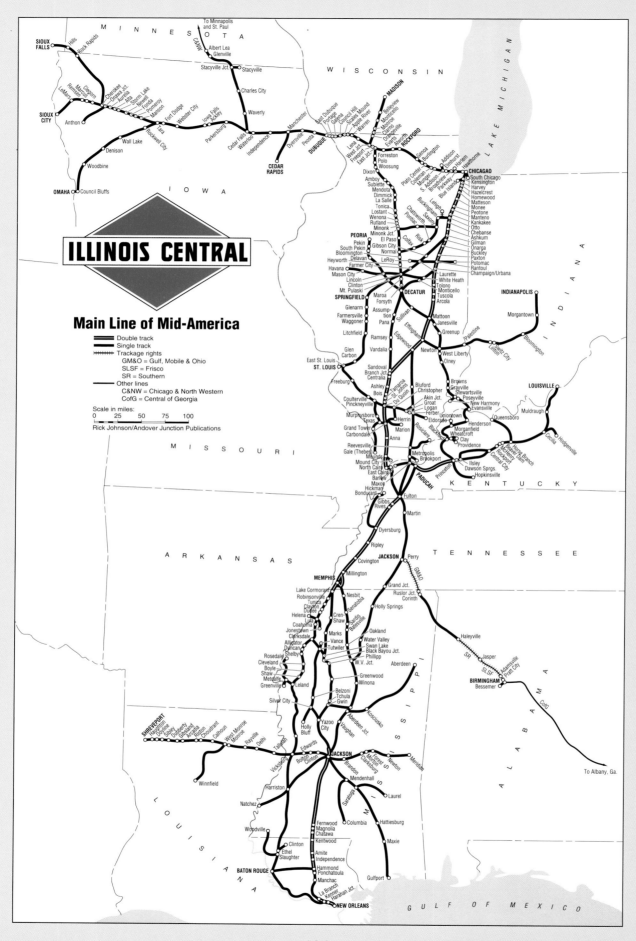

Main Line of Mid-America

Double track
Single track
Trackage rights
GM&O = Gulf, Mobile & Ohio
SLSF = Frisco
SR = Southern
Other lines
C&NW = Chicago & North Western
CofG = Central of Georgia

Scale in miles:
0 25 50 75 100

Rick Johnson/Andover Junction Publications

cess would be elimination of redundant lines.

Over the next dozen years, ICG would create far more railroads than it had absorbed. It began slowly with C&G "unmerging" to become an independent again in October 1975. A year later the Illinois Central Industries holding company announced its plans to shed ICG from its portfolio. In 1978 Southern Railway took a serious look at ICG as a merger partner and then rejected it in 1979. ICG was now not only unprofitable but unwanted.

In February 1981 the Madison Branch was sold to the year-old Chicago, Madison & Northern. CM&N perished to become the Central Wisconsin, which later became the Wisconsin & Calumet—which in the 1990's ended up running *Panama*-colored F-units pulling *Panama*-colored passenger trains made up of former IC cars!

The flood gates opened in 1984, and over the next few years the 109-mile Albert Lea line became the Cedar Valley; the Gulf & Mississippi took over 713 miles of the GM&O south of Corinth; Chicago Central & Pacific took over 704 miles of the Iowa Division; Paducah & Louisville bought the 282-mile Kentucky Division; MidSouth acquired 418 miles of IC from Meridian to Shreveport and Gulfport; and Chicago, Missouri & Western took over 633 miles of ex-GM&O lines from Joliet to Kansas City and St. Louis. Other ICG parcels became the West Tennessee, the Tennken and the Indiana Rail Road, and some segments were sold to Indiana Hi-Rail, Southern and Seaboard System. By 1988 the 9,400-mile ICG was down to a 2,900-mile spine from Chicago to New Orleans.

IC Industries renamed itself the Whitman Corporation after its chocolate candy subsidiary and in 1989 sold the railroad to the Prospect Group, which had created the Mid-South. Prospect quickly sold MidSouth and renamed the ICG back to "Illinois Central." The steam-era black-and-white livery returned with the name, but the green diamond was missing, having been sold with the Iowa Division to Chicago Central in 1985. The new IC's modern graphic of the 1972 ICG I-Ball was quickly dubbed the "Death Star" for its resemblance to Darth Vader's base in *Star Wars*.

The new IC fixed up its physical plant (reducing the famous double-track speedway to well-maintained single track) and quickly repainted its locomotive fleet into the new black scheme. It has been heralded as a textbook example of modern survival and success.

Someday I'll have to spend some time on it.

WHEN ILLINOIS CENTRAL GULF began to unravel in the 1980's, the Chicago Central & Pacific not only picked up nearly the entire Iowa Division but also bought the rights to the green diamond herald, which was worn by a pair of CC&P ex-IC Paducah Geeps (left) at Council Bluffs, Iowa, in August 1990. Thus, when the Prospect Group bought the remains of the ICG from the successor to IC Industries in 1989, the reborn "Illinois Central" had to come up with a new herald. The new "Death Star" graphic adorned traditional IC black and white colors (below) on an ex-GM&O SD40 at Valley Junction in East St. Louis in June 1990. Locomotive numbers appeared in a different style of lettering than the IC of yore, but with the return of the black-suite garb and the white chassis stripe, the "feel" of that early diesel-era IC was back again.

The Disappearin' Railroad Blues

The end came for the Gruber on a cold and snowy December 21, 1985, when ICG Extra 8045 North ran from La Salle to Freeport as the last train on the line through Dixon. The Geep was running backward, and the crew was made up of men that I'd worked with: Conductor Packy McDonald, engineer Harley Austen and brakemen Bobby Linden and Howard Sheppard. It was their last run, too, as all four were taking severance.

Chet French had already elected to go with the new Chicago Central where smaller crews and new work rules made the familiar railroad and equipment seem strangely different. It seemed unreal even as I wrote about it for *Railfan & Railroad* Magazine in my office in Newton, New Jersey.

I had watched close-up as Conrail had made a shambles of the Northeast and then brought it out of the darkness behind a parade of clean, bright "dress blue" diesels. But I had been spared the gory details of the transformation of the Illinois Central. It is sufficient to know that Chicago Central has some pretty red Paducah Geeps with green diamond heralds still sitting beside the turntable at Wallace and that my orange SD40A's are now painted steam-era black on the new Main Line of Mid-America. I really will have to make an effort to photograph them someday.

But after visiting Dixon in the summer of 1987 and seeing the Seventh Street crossing with no tracks, I know that I can never go home again. That world is gone forever.

It's sad, but not tragic. It's railroading in the '90's. It's the world of Amtrak and double-stacks and FREDs instead of cabooses. It's super cabs and Super Fleets and Susquehanna SD45's. It's also the world of Union Pacific 4-6-6-4 3985 hauling a Domeliner over Sherman Hill, and Andy Muller latching out on his Blue Mountain & Reading T1 4-8-4 with 40 loads of tidewater-bound anthracite coal at Port Clinton. I've found the world of steam that had eluded me in my youth.

There's still a lot of railroading out there and all sorts of opportunities. The new experiences don't displace the older ones, they just add more layers to the memories. It's enough to know that they happened. Of course, a few well-exposed Ektachromes don't hurt.

Today no camera gets between me and the *City of New Orleans* accelerating grandly southward out of Champaign in the brilliant winter sun with A-B-A E-units responding to the throttle, one notch at a time . . . or Benny Beirau waving "drive 'em" . . . or black Geeps struggling up La Salle hill . . . or Bob Morgridge stringing those grade-crossing whistles all together with a 2100.

Nobody can merge those memories out of existence or tear up their tracks through time. ⬧

YOU CAN GO HOME again, but you won't find the railroad. Though the Dixon freighthouse remained essentially unchanged in the summer of 1987, the tracks of the Gruber were gone, and the yard was full of weeds. Today, a truck garage fills this scene, and the freighthouse has vanished. Maybe this book will help us all to remember what the Illinois Central meant to Dixon and other IC communities—and to those of us who grew up in an Illinois Central hometown.